'Has there ever been a time when the [...]re
visible to the world? This excellent bo[...]ell
as inspiration, to those who aspire to [...]p.
It helpfully roots the book in the Bibl[...]al
insights from the authors' lived experie[...]. I expect to be coming back to this
book time and again to provoke, inspire and shape my thoughts and actions for
the benefit of the common good. As such, I am delighted to commend it to you.'
Alastair Bateman, CEO, Church Mission Society

'By combining their personal stories and diverse expertise, Simon Barrington
and Justin Humphreys have provided a feast of insight and reflection on what
just leadership looks like – and how to put it into practice. This will be a valuable
and accessible resource to any who are involved in leading organizations and
shaping their culture. It is an important contribution towards helping us to
build safer, healthier churches, organizations and communities – shaped by the
priorities of God's kingdom.'
The Rt Reverend Dr Jonathan Gibbs, Church of England Lead Bishop for
Safeguarding

'Leadership matters – I have more books on leadership on my shelves than almost
any other category – but too often what passes as leadership seems to have lost its
soul. To have Simon and Justin centre their contribution so clearly and helpfully
in the character of God is both refreshing and inspiring. I cannot recommend it
too highly.'
Paul Harcourt, National Leader, New Wine England

'This book is empowering. Reminding us that justice is at the very heart of who
God is, and the cry of the world that he has made, *Just Leadership* is packed with
practical advice to help us to lead more justly. It will enable willing leaders to
uncover the unseen prejudices of their hearts and to challenge and dismantle
the injustices lurking in the cultures of their churches or organizations. It is
this dual focus, with its practical application, that makes this book so powerful.'
Simon Harris and Ceri Harris, burlington.church (Ipswich, UK)

'I cannot think of a time when a just leadership would be more relevant or
applicable. In a world of profiles and soundbites, Simon and Justin get to the
very heart of godly character. Filled with biblical and psychological wisdom, this
is a book that should be on the shelves of every leader today.'
The Reverend Will van der Hart, Co-director, The Mind & Soul Foundation

'I have underlined something in almost every paragraph in this book. There's
something vital and so important for us all to understand and share on every
page. I want to reread and reflect on every one of these nuggets. This book has

given me a deeper understanding of how *justice* is at the heart of who God is and how we need to live this out in our everyday lives.'
Michele Hawthorne, founder and Director, Press Red

'In this book we find a model for just leadership in a world longing to hear a better story than "returning to normal", and the tools to make it happen when so often we are stuck for what to do. We are reminded that to seek justice, love mercy and walk humbly with God can mean examining and challenging in ways that can be unsettling and uncomfortable. I cannot cheer its sentiments without applying its challenge to my own life; I cannot expect others to be just leaders without using this book to search my own world-view, motivation, actions, relationships and ambition. Our encouragement in this endeavour, as this book reminds us, is that our Saviour has gone to those dark, difficult places before us and calls us to follow him to heal the brokenness of our world.'
Ross Hendry, CEO, Spurgeons Childcare

'This book will change the way you lead. Its biblical, theological mandate for leaders to pursue justice is moving, inspiring and potentially life-changing. The world that God made and loves needs leaders who will seek wholeheartedly to live and exercise leadership justly. *Just Leadership* will help you to see why and will show you how.'
The Rt Reverend Dr Emma Ineson, Bishop of Penrith

'This book is dangerous but in a great way. It leaves no stone unturned in its quest to help its readers to become just leaders. Just fabulous; challenging and inspiring – I will be buying copies for all my team.'
The Venerable Rhiannon King, Archdeacon, Ipswich, and Director, Inspiring Ipswich

'I have known Simon for many years and been the recipient of his wisdom and understanding of justice and development of leaders, myself included. Simon's commitment to following Jesus, his heart for justice and passion for raising up leaders of influence and godly character is inspiring in itself. This book is a must-read for anyone who is serious about tackling injustices in society today.'
Dr John Kirkby CBE, founder, Christians Against Poverty

'This book is a must-read for leaders and aspiring leaders of any kind. In a world where we, all too often, see those we have mistakenly placed on pedestals fall dramatically to the ground, Simon's and Justin's wisdom and passion for just leaders could not be more relevant. The Church is meant to be a light on a hill, reflecting the glory and goodness and justice of God. If we are to shine, as we are called to, we cannot afford to ignore the challenges contained within these pages. It is time to dig deep, to consider our motivations and to seek after God and not

our own desires and security. *Just Leadership* is all the better for practising what it preaches. Its wisdom is birthed in vulnerability. I believe that it will challenge and inspire you in equal measure. What it won't do is leave you unmoved.'
Bekah Legg, Director, Restored

'*Just Leadership* is full of helpful questions, lessons and wisdom for all Christian leaders. Although they do not claim to have all the answers, Simon Barrington's and Justin Humphreys' vulnerability in sharing their own leadership stories make this book a wide-ranging and helpful manual for any leader seeking to lead from a place of authentic justice-seeking.'
Chine McDonald, Head of Public Engagement, Christian Aid

'What a welcome contribution to leadership studies and to the movements for social justice! Barrington and Humphreys offer a robust, theological study of justice itself – rooted in who God is and how God acts, manifested in God's grace for us and flowing from God into us in all our relationships – that exhorts leaders to play their part in nurturing such a robust culture of justice. So much of this splendid book brings together real life with theoretical study. With so many studies of leadership appearing annually, it is hard to think of one that says something fresh, but *Just Leadership* does. A real godsend.'
The Reverend Canon Dr Scot McKnight and Laura Barringer, co-authors, *A Church Called Tov*

'*Just Leadership* is not so much a book as a catalyst for change – in leadership culture but also in the heart of us as leaders. In it, we are reminded that God-honouring leadership has the potential to create ripples of justice across homes, churches and society. If you want to build a healthy culture where character is valued more highly than competence, and where learning from and empowering others is at the heart of your mission, this book will be a game-changer for you. Honest, hope-filled and packed with practical tools for leaders to use, *Just Leadership* is the book on integrity, inclusion and intentionality that every team needs to read.'
Cathy Madavan, speaker, writer and broadcaster

'Simon and Justin have written a book that is compelling and practical, that draws on their own leadership and life journeys. It is timely, biblical, honest and, above all, applicable to anyone in leadership. I commend this book to every leader and am sure that it will inspire, challenge and inform in a way that will cause readers to consider justice as a framework for their leadership.'
Mark Markiewicz, CEO of CWR, Waverley Abbey Trust

'This is an inspiring book on an often overlooked aspect of leadership. Thought provoking and thorough, it will offer a framework for pondering and praying into your own character, as well as giving a wider perspective on your leadership. In a time when calls for justice are increasingly urgent and acute, this book is a timely reminder of our call and responsibility to uphold and promote justice as leaders, and an opportunity to take the time to consider this carefully, guided by authors rooted in a great deal of personal experience and passion. It is a book not to rush through, but to read, put down, pray, pick up again, pray some more . . . expect it to unsettle, to challenge and to change the way you lead.'

Dr Kate Middleton, founder and Co-director, The Mind & Soul Foundation

'This book is a powerful fusion of personal lessons learnt, theological insight and leadership principles that provoke and challenge us to lead differently for the sake of others and the change needed in our world. It's a call to slow down as leaders, to listen, to begin to understand, then to speak and act with, and on behalf of, others.'

Tim Morfin, founder and CEO, Transforming Lives for Good (TLG)

'This is both a timely and necessary book for churches, charities and businesses as we collectively aim to pursue justice, integrity and transparency, and become leaders who can model what it means to prioritize Kingdom values. Simon and Justin provide not just a biblical argument but also helpful, researched and pragmatic guidance based on their collective experience. This book provides a helpful framework through which leaders can cultivate a more secure sense of identity and a deep sense of connection with those around them.'

Gareth Russell, Managing Director, Jersey Road PR

'At this unique moment in history, the Church is faced with a crucial choice. Will we lead the way when it comes to tackling injustice or will we perpetuate the systems and structures that enable it to flourish? This book is a must-read for any leaders committed to placing God's heart for justice at the centre of their life, their leadership and their organization. Sharing profound personal experience, coupled with invaluable professional expertise, Simon and Justin address the uncomfortable barriers and blind spots that can prevent us from seeing injustice, and challenge the leadership deficiencies that can hold us back from dealing with the roots of injustice when they are exposed. Offering practical strategies, tools and insights, this book will encourage all leaders to become more attuned to God's passion for justice and enable them to act decisively, speak out courageously and stand alongside victims and survivors of injustice with greater compassion and empathy. *Just Leadership* is a timely and much needed resource for those of us desiring to lead the way in the fight for justice, hoping for meaningful change and longing to make a lasting difference to the inequality we see in the world around us.'

Nicki Sims, Senior Leader, Skylark International

'With prophetic clarity and practical instruction, Simon and Justin have offered us a drink of water for our thirsty collective souls. There is no longer any doubt that this cultural moment is a blazing light of exposure, revealing deep injustices and inequities that flourish through toxic leadership. Rather than settling for an indictment of the status quo, Simon and Justin offer us a way forward. They lead us not to drink of the gall of our current state but offer instead a healing balm that could cure us and lead us from despair to life. Read this book and then rethink everything else. I promise, it's the best of news.'
Danielle Strickland, author, speaker, trainer and global social justice advocate

'If you are looking primarily to increase your head knowledge and acquire new skills, then this book is not for you, because this is about your head, heart and soul. It is about each of us as whole embodied people, yet interdependent as the Body of Christ. This is an accessible book in its style and presentation, yet is deeply challenging. As you engage with the pages, you will be transformed as you are invited to live an ever-stronger "yes" to participating in God's kingdom work of transformation as you pray "your kingdom come on earth as in heaven".'
The Rt Reverend Rachel Treweek, Bishop of Gloucester, Lead Bishop for HM Prisons

'This book is a call to action for every leader. A call to willingly and courageously lay down the broken and dysfunctional leadership behaviours that many of us have learnt from the generations before us and be prepared to model something different. *Just Leadership* asks us to bravely examine ourselves and choose to value character over charisma, authenticity over popularity and relationship over reach. Rooted in biblical truth, Simon and Justin inspire a vision of what our world will look like when we live and learn to "act justly, love mercy and walk humbly with God" (Micah 6.8).'
Arianna Walker, speaker, author and CEO, Mercy UK

Simon Barrington is the founder and Director of Forge Leadership Consultancy, an organization that is focused on raising up a generation of leaders of character and influence. He is also a co-founder of WeAreCompany, which helps to strengthen the quality of leaders' relationships in organizations, charities and churches. In addition, he is the author (with Rachel Luetchford) of *Leading – The Millennial Way* (SPCK, 2019).

Simon studied physics and music at Cardiff University before becoming a senior manager at BT, then was seconded to the Cabinet Office. In 2003, he became the Executive Director of Samarian's Purse, a post he held for more than 13 years, leading emergency relief and development initiatives across the world. During this time, Simon studied for a Masters in Global Leadership at Fuller Theological College, California. Simon now lives in the East of England, attends a Baptist church, has been married for 31 years and has two adult children.

Justin Humphreys is joint Chief Executive of the independent Christian safeguarding charity thirtyone:eight, based in the UK. He is also Honorary Lecturer in the Department of Applied Psychology at the University of Chester. He has had a career in social work, social welfare and church leadership spanning more than 25 years.

Justin currently chairs the Christian Forum for Safeguarding, a collaborative forum for the national safeguarding leads from many of Christian denominations and networks across the UK. He is also the founder (alongside Sarah Champion MP) of the All Party Parliamentary Group on Safeguarding in Faith Settings and is co-author of *Escaping the Maze of Spiritual Abuse: Creating Healthy Christian Cultures* (SPCK, 2019) with Dr Lisa Oakley.

Justin holds an MSc in Child Protection and Strategic Management (Edinburgh Napier University) and a BSc (Hons) in Social Work Studies (Birmingham City University). Justin lives in the South West of England and has been married for 28 years with three adult children.

JUST LEADERSHIP

Putting integrity and justice at the
heart of how you lead

Simon Barrington and Justin Humphreys

First published in Great Britain in 2021

Society for Promoting Christian Knowledge
36 Causton Street
London SW1P 4ST
www.spck.org.uk

British Library Cataloguing-in-Publication Data
A catalogue record for this book is available from the British Library

ISBN 978–0–281–08553–8
eBook ISBN 978–0–281–08560–6

1 3 5 7 9 10 8 6 4 2

Typeset by Manila Typesetting Company
First printed in Great Britain by Ashford Colour Press

eBook by Manila Typesetting Company

Produced on paper from sustainable forests

Contents

This is what the Lord Almighty said:
'Administer true justice; show mercy
and compassion to one another.
Do not oppress the widow or the
fatherless, the foreigner or the poor.
Do not plot evil against each other.'

(ZECHARIAH 7.9–10)

Preface

Justice is the heart cry of the next generation. A call for a fairer, more transparent, more equal society where everyone can play their part.

It's a call to tackle the injustices of the past and to stand up for truth, to stand up for freedom and to champion the cause of victims, the marginalized and the powerless.

It's a cry that comes from and resonates with the heart of God. It's who God *is* and what God *does*. But is it at the heart of who we are and how we lead?

Of course, much has been written over the years about this cause. In many ways it's nothing new and the verses at the beginning of this preface would indicate that it's a direction that has been calling us for thousands of years and is embodied in both the New Testament and the Old Testament.

So why does it feel as if we're living through a time of increased injustices? Of #MeToo and the explosion of sexual abuse scandals in the Church and wider society to name some examples?

This book was written during lockdown and recovery from the coronavirus global pandemic. A pandemic that laid bare further inequalities in society that were brought into stark relief by the statistics at the peak of the outbreak in the UK.

Nick Stripe, Head of Health Analysis at the UK Government's Office for National Statistics, commented:

> People living in more deprived areas have experienced COVID-19 mortality rates more than double those living in less deprived areas. General mortality rates are normally higher in more deprived areas, but so far COVID-19 appears to be taking them higher still.[1]

It's not only poverty that increases inequality and injustice, though, with race also a key factor in the mortality rate among those contracting coronavirus. A study by the Institute for Fiscal Studies shows that, in the UK, 'After stripping out the role of age and geography, Bangladeshi hospital fatalities are twice those of the white British group, Pakistani deaths are 2.9 times as high and black African deaths 3.7 times as high.'[2]

The pandemic has also increased levels of concern about domestic abuse, with the charity Refuge reporting that phone calls to its helpline have increased by 25 per cent and access to its Internet services has increased by 150 per cent.

What about children at such a time as this? In many ways they are more vulnerable than ever. They are seen less and heard less. As with others experiencing domestic abuse, children are being held captive in the very places where they are being systematically abused, with reduced ability to escape and call for help. The National Society for the Prevention of Cruelty to Children (NSPCC) has reported exponential increases in calls to ChildLine from young people during the pandemic, citing physical, emotional and sexual abuse and an alarming rise in concerns about mental well-being among the most common reasons for calls.

> We are hearing from children who have been cut off from vital support networks such as school, and friends, and that has increased their feelings of loneliness and vulnerability. They may have pre-existing mental health issues which are exacerbated by the current crisis.[3]

Changes to the ways we work have brought their challenges too. In our race to explore new means of maintaining contact in this new pandemic-driven climate, we see a new phenomenon. The rapid migration from physical contact to virtual contact via online platforms has resulted in further increases in risk for children (and some adults) as churches, charities and others scramble to reinvent their models of service delivery. For some of them, this has unwittingly opened up new opportunities for those who are motivated to exploit children, young people and others by any means possible.

Of course, there are endless examples of injustice that we could cite as relevant throughout the pages of this book. What we discuss is by no means an exhaustive commentary and we humbly ask for your forgiveness if the issues that most resonate with you are not covered. We are, however, sure that the principles we discuss are transferable and applicable in most, if not all, contexts. We write from our own personal and professional perspectives and offer this as a beginning to enable you to explore a broader range of concerns.

Justice, though, is about more than the causes themselves. It's about who we are as leaders and who we are becoming.

The key question we try to answer in this book is not 'What just causes should I choose to champion and fight for?' but 'How can I become the type of leader who can be used by God to tackle these injustices?' How can I develop to be the type of leader who will tackle systemic abuses of power; who will be courageous and selfless in speaking up and standing out at such a time as this, and a leader who will inspire others to do the same?

It's time to pause and ask some big questions.

⟨What does God require of me at this time? What kind of leader does he desire me to be?⟨⟨

Dare we dream of the kinds of organizations that may emerge and be bold enough to imagine the nature of the influence we could have on society as a result of leading from a heart for justice?

In the following chapters, we set out a framework to explore the detail of what it means not only to lead *for* justice but also to lead *with* justice in a variety of settings with God's heart for justice at the centre of it all. We then expand on the behaviours, values and actions that we believe are critical to the formation and practice of *just leadership* and challenge us all to be more considered, purposeful and deliberate in our efforts as we build our organizations and respond to a range of injustices in society.

As we emerge from the biggest global shock to our economy, way of life and health in over a century, what kind of future do we want, what kind of legacy do we want to leave and what kind of leaders will shape it?

We believe that we have a moment in time to galvanize and champion the rise of a generation of leaders who say **enough is enough,** and who build together the foundations of a just society because they themselves model justice in all their interactions, behaviours and relationships.

This book sets out a model of leadership that has justice and fairness right at its heart.

We believe this is *just leadership*.

Simon Barrington and Justin Humphreys

Acknowledgments

Justin would like to thank all those who have contributed to the many learning opportunities he has had over the past 25 years, some of which have been explored in the pages of this book. Special thanks go to Hayley who has been a steadfast guide and loving balance for the past 28 years.

Simon would like to acknowledge the formative role that Fuller Seminary has played in his thinking on justice and leadership and to thank the many colleagues and friends who have also helped shape and form these ideas into the pages of this book through rich interactions, dialogue and shared experiences. Above all I would not have been able to write this book without the constant love, companionship, and care of Heather for the past 31 years, to whom I want to give special thanks and deep appreciation.

Part I
JUST . . .

Introduction to Part I

This book is divided into three main sections. In this first section, we address the basis for all that follows.

First, that our focus and blueprint for *just leadership* – putting integrity and justice at the heart of how we lead – must begin with our understanding of who God is.

Second, that we understand the fundamental importance of our leadership and our identities being rooted in God and reflecting God.

Finally, that all we do is achieved through our relational connectedness to each other.

God is the one who satisfies the passion for justice, the longing for spirituality, the hunger for relationship, the yearning for beauty. And God, the true God, is the God we see in Jesus of Nazareth, Israel's Messiah, the world's true Lord.[1]

N. T. WRIGHT

1

Just God

SIMON BARRINGTON AND JUSTIN HUMPHREYS

This book is not a theological treatise on justice or on leadership. It is, in many ways, a practical handbook for leading justly in our current environment. However, it is a book that is rooted theologically and biblically and although neither of us is a trained theologian, we take the issue of grounding this work in this way extremely seriously.

Many a theological treatise has been written on biblical justice and we would point you to several excellent resources that will allow you to take your thinking further in understanding this whole area. We have been influenced by Chris Wright's *The Mission of God*, Tim Keller's *Generous Justice*, Ken Wytsma's *Pursuing Justice* and *The Grand Paradox*, Gary Haugen's *Just Courage* and *Good News About Injustice*, Tearfund's resource *Live Justly*, Ben Lindsay's *We Need to Talk about Race* and many of Tom Wright's books on the subject, among many others.

Our particular focus as we start our journey into *just leadership* is to look biblically at Jesus as a leader and how justice shaped his character and his ministry, mission and purpose.

We do this not just by looking at some proof texts and expounding them to fit our narrative but, rather, by looking at the broad sweep of the biblical story and seeing how justice created the foundations for Jesus' leadership, shaped the nature of his leadership and therefore can give us a framework for a Bible-centred, Jesus-centred, justice-centred leadership.

Before we get to that, though, what do we mean by *just leadership* and why should we care?

What do we mean by *just leadership*?

To get to *just leadership*, let's first explore what we mean by justice. Justice, as defined in the *Cambridge English Dictionary* is: 'fairness in the way that people are dealt with'. However, as Gary Haugen offers:

> Although the dictionary is supposed to tell us the meaning of words, every word is defined only by other words . . . *Life* is a word, but a dictionary can tell us next to nothing about the 'meaning of life'. Likewise, a meaningful understanding of 'justice' or of a 'just God' does not emerge from a neat all-purpose definition of the word *justice*.[2]

If we only used the dictionary definition, then we probably wouldn't need to write a book, but just encourage leaders to get on with dealing with people fairly!

But what does fairness mean? What one person considers fair, others may consider unfair.

What benchmark for fairness or justice are we using?

Rather than start with a dictionary definition, we want to start theologically, taking the whole of Scripture initially and then focusing in on Jesus. Our task is to make God's justice our jumping off point and our single lens and reference point throughout.

The first stage is to see justice as who God *is* and what God *does*. It is the very nature of God's character and is a key driver in his actions throughout the existence of the universe.

Ultimately, we will see from our broad sweep of the biblical narrative that God's justice is about restoring broken relationships. Our relationship with God, our relationship with ourselves, our relationship with others and our relationship with creation.[3]

Following on from this definition of justice, we begin to see that *just leadership* means participation in the restoration of those broken relationships and the purposeful intervention in the systems, processes, beliefs and constructs that create injustice, inequality, exploitation and oppression. It's not only a leadership that *does* justice, though. It is a leadership that *is* just, has loving kindness at its heart, that hates evil, that is generous, that is active, courageous, humble, faithful and that uses all power for good.

Just leadership goes further than just tackling social injustice and restoring broken relationships between people – although that is a core component – and seeks to join in with God's restorative justice mission to reconcile all people to himself and to renew creation through *the way that we lead.*

Why should we care about *just leadership*?

As suggested above, we should care about justice and what it means to be a just leader because this will lead us to a deeper understanding of who God is. One leads to the other. If we understand anything of God, then we understand what justice looks like. If we understand something about justice, then we are seeing an undeniable part of the character of God or, as Ken Wytsma puts it: 'Engagement in justice and our worship and knowledge of God are inextricable.'[4] Ultimately, we care about *just leadership* because Jesus does and because he is, without doubt, our best example of this.

Biblical overview

The following section is a rapid overview of some of the key themes throughout Scripture that underpin the broad biblical story. We can't do it full justice here, but we hope that it will whet your appetite to delve deeper into this subject and to get your Bible out and start reading. We have followed an outline that we have found extremely helpful from the organization JustLove, who work extensively with students to promote a justice-centred life.[5]

It may be that you're seeing this overview of the Bible for the first time or it may be that you have read or heard it thousands of times before. Either way, we encourage you to look at the story of Scripture with fresh eyes, searching for the central theme of leading with justice throughout.

Just foundations

In the beginning . . .

The creation narrative is our starting point and gives us a wonderful picture of a world where everything works as it should do, where everything is in its right place, where there is full harmony between Creator and created and where there is true and full shalom. It's a picture of God as the Creator of a just world – a glimpse of our past and of our future.

In the narrative of Genesis chapters 1 and 2:

> We find the repeated refrain of 'it was good', climaxing in the pronouncement of the whole of creation being 'very good' (Gen. 1.31). Indeed, the very first chapter of the Bible paints an image for us of a 'good' creation, a creation of justice, of the flourishing of creation – filling the spaces, with good rule established in those spaces. We might describe this vision of creation in Genesis 1 as reverberating with harmony.[6]

The creation picture widens our view of what justice means. Not just fairness for people but also creation restored, harmony restored. Shalom. Reverberating with harmony. Or, as Glenn Smith puts it, '*shalom* is where justice and peace embrace'.[7]

Rebellion

That shalom didn't last for very long, though. Just as soon as God had created shalom, rebellion entered from stage left (Genesis 3—4).

This rebellion broke the harmonious relationship between God and us, between people and between us and creation – and caused untold chaos, discord and pain. In a devastating way. Almost immediately, injustice enters as a consequence of sin and we begin to read of Cain and Abel, of war and familial breakdown. A pattern that would repeat and worsen.

God's big plan, therefore, is and has always been to create something perfect (or 'very good') and keep it that way. The rebellion of the fall and all that followed necessitated a determined show of God's love for creation that has continued ever since, right up to today. This was exemplified in the life and death of Jesus, whose mission was to lead us back to God and restore the world order as his Father had intended it:

> Jesus' mission, in his life as well as in his death and resurrection, was to bring about a world made new – a world made right – to initiate

the process of restoring the whole creation, bringing it back in line with how God intended it to be.[8]

More of that in a moment . . .

The promise

God's great redemption plan for the whole of mankind begins with a promise. It starts with God calling Abraham and emerges as a plan to call a whole people – a nation under God's rule and reign. God makes a covenant – a promise – with Abraham, an eternal promise of faithfulness and a commitment that the nations of the whole earth will be blessed through him (Genesis 12.3). A promise that justice will come for all people.

Israel rescued from injustice

First, though, God's people must suffer their own injustice.

The story of the exodus is rooted in Israel's history and is a story of God's people being oppressed foreigners without a future, without a purpose, suffering injustice at the hands of the Egyptians. And so, woven into the Biblical narrative, is not only the *concept* of liberation and justice but also the *lived experience* of the chosen people of God.

As Mike Kelly, Partnership Manager at Biblica, reflects:

So, we see very thoroughly as the exodus narrative begins that the pattern of the restoration of justice, of shalom, is grounded in God; in this way the attention of Israel to justice, to shalom, is tied to their understanding of their history with God. The exodus and liberation from an oppressive situation will be a constant refrain in Israel's literary reflections on her history. They were oppressed foreigners, enslaved without hope by a power far greater than themselves. Their only hope for justice must come from God, who is the author of justice. God indeed responds to their cries arising from oppression and in the signal miracle of the Old Testament liberates Israel from slavery.[9]

This is a practical story with a practical outcome that has given hope and motivation to the people of God in marginalized situations in countless countries over twenty centuries. A real-life demonstration that the promise of a narrative of justice restored is real and tangible.

Rules and regulations

To the people of Israel, liberated from slavery in Egypt, God then gave a set of ceremonial and social laws that regulated almost every aspect of Jewish life – from morals to ceremonies, to the government, army, criminal justice, commerce, marriage and social relationships. It also provided for the welfare of widows, orphans, the poor and foreigners.

As Tim Keller puts it:

> Even in the seemingly boring rules and regulations of tabernacle rituals, we see that God cares about the poor, that his laws make provision for the disadvantaged. God's concern for justice permeated every part of Israel's life. It should also permeate our lives.[10]

The warnings and the foretelling

The Old Testament prophets were God's spokespeople – and they spoke out against injustice, keeping their harshest words and sternest warnings for those who were oppressors, who acted unjustly and who would not amend their ways.

> For if you truly amend your ways and your doings, if you truly execute justice one with another, if you do not oppress the alien, the fatherless or the widow, or shed innocent blood . . . then I will let you dwell in this place, in the land that I gave of old to your fathers forever.
> (Jeremiah 7.5–7, RSV)

> Because you trample upon the poor and take from him exactions of wheat, you have built houses of hewn stone, but you shall not dwell in them . . . For I know how many are your transgressions, and how great are your sins – you who afflict the righteous, who take a bribe, and turn aside the needy in the gate.
> (Amos 5.11–12, RSV)

Yet there was always the promise of restoration, the promise of justice and mercy.

> In that day . . . I will abolish the bow, the sword, and war from the land; and I will make you lie down in safety. And I will betroth you to me forever; I will betroth you to me in righteousness and in justice, in steadfast love, and in mercy.
> (Hosea 2.16–19, RSV)

Ultimately, the prophets pointed to a Messiah who would bring justice not just to Israel itself but also to all the nations:

> 'Here is my servant, whom I uphold,
>   my chosen one in whom I delight;
> I will put my Spirit on him,
>   and he will bring justice to the nations.
> He will not shout or cry out,
>   or raise his voice in the streets.
> A bruised reed he will not break,
>   and a smouldering wick he will not snuff out.
> In faithfulness he will bring forth justice;
>   he will not falter or be discouraged
> till he establishes justice on earth.
>   In his teaching the islands will put their hope.'
> (Isaiah 42.1–4)

It is the foreshadowed Messiah to whom we now turn, the one who will not falter or be discouraged until he establishes justice on earth, and in whom we all put our hope.

Jesus – the centre of it all

What has been foreshadowed in the Old Testament, now comes to fruition in Jesus. His ministry, which is hallmarked by justice, with a purpose to bring about justice and with a future that will usher in the fullness of shalom, a new creation and the fulfilment of the law and the prophets, is the perfect example for us as leaders. In his life on earth, Jesus demonstrates clearly how to lead as a justice-fulfilling, justice-centred leader by providing an alternative narrative to that of rebellion, destruction and the lust for power.

As Ben Lindsay puts it in his book *We Need to Talk about Race*, 'Whether racial injustice (Luke 10.30–37), class prejudice (Luke 17.11–19) or gender discrimination (John 4.1–42), in Jesus Christ we have the perfect example of how to challenge intolerance.'[11]

Just ministry

Jesus left us in no doubt that justice was at the heart of his ministry. It couldn't be clearer. We don't have to read into parables or interpret stories; it's there in his own words, as he echoes the justice call of the prophets and proclaims that today this prophecy comes to fruition.

> He went to Nazareth, where he had been brought up, and on the Sabbath day he went into the synagogue, as was his custom. He stood up to read, and the scroll of the prophet Isaiah was handed to him. Unrolling it, he found the place where it is written:
> 'The Spirit of the Lord is on me,
>> because he has anointed me
>> to proclaim good news to the poor.
> He has sent me to proclaim freedom for the prisoners
>> and recovery of sight for the blind,
> to set the oppressed free, to proclaim the year of the Lord's favour.'
> Then he rolled up the scroll, gave it back to the attendant and sat down. The eyes of everyone in the synagogue were fastened on him. He began by saying to them, 'Today this scripture is fulfilled in your hearing.
> (Luke 4.16–20)

Justice is a huge theme of what Jesus *said* – centring around his teachings on love – love for God and neighbour, love that reaches across social boundaries, love even for enemies.

Justice is also a huge theme in what Jesus *did*. From his birth to his death, Jesus lived with victims of injustice, and he was a victim of injustice.[12]

Jesus reached out to people at the margins, to victims and survivors, to people at the lowest levels of society – the outcast and the maligned. His approach was revolutionary for the Near East and turned culture upside down.

Just purpose

Ultimately, as we touched on earlier in this chapter, Jesus came to fulfil God's whole purpose (Acts 20.27) and the cross was at the centre of doing exactly that.[13]

> So, the cross was the unavoidable cost of God's mission. But it is equally true and biblical to say that the cross is the unavoidable centre of our mission. All Christian mission flows from the cross – as its source, its power, and as that which defines its scope. It is vital that we see the cross as central and integral to every aspect of holistic, biblical mission, that is of all we do in the name of the crucified and risen Jesus.[14]

As we have seen, that mission and purpose has at its heartbeat a desire for justice. Only in the cross is justice fulfilled. Only in the dealing with the guilt of sin, once and for all, only in the defeat of the powers of evil, only in the destruction of death, only in our being reconciled to God and to one another, is the character of God, with a heart of justice, revealed.

When all is said and done, every just outcome exists because of the cross. Every injustice is removed because of the cross. That is the total scope of God's redemptive work.

We dare not tackle injustice alone. We dare not take on this mantle of *just leadership* and think that we can defeat the evils of injustices everywhere in our own strength. We dare not lift up this banner, except that the cross is lifted high as the centrality of our lives and our hope.

Just future

So, where does all this lead us to? What do we make of this challenge to face injustice and what difference might we expect from it as we look forwards and into the fray? As Tom Wright puts it:

If we believe that in the end God will put all things right, will 'do justice' in that positive, creative, healing, restorative sense; and if we believe that when God raised Jesus from the dead he did exactly that, close up and personal, in the one human being who represented and stood in for everyone else – then we cannot hold back from the imperative to 'do justice', in this full sense, at every opportunity in our world. In the power of the Spirit, we must name and shame the injustices that are still rampant, and work for their abolition. And we must take care that in our personal lives, and particularly in the lives of our churches themselves, injustice is rooted out as far and wide as can be done. Only if we are doing this will it make any sense to preach and teach about God's new creation, about the way in which Jesus' resurrection resonates out into the renewal, the putting-right, of creation.[15]

Beslan

This biblical understanding of justice may make sense in theory, but it can be much harder to see it work out in practice, in a world full of hurting, horrors and heartbreak. One such horror was the Beslan school siege, which started on 1 September 2004, lasted three days, involved the illegal imprisonment of more than 1,000 people as hostages and ended with the deaths of 331 people – including 186 children.[16] The siege was undertaken by a group of armed Chechen separatists who occupied School Number One in the town of Beslan, North Ossetia. On the third day, Russian security forces stormed the building, releasing many hostages, but the ensuing violence killed nearly one-third of the hostages.

It's hard to overstate the horror, outrage and anger in the local community and globally that innocent people should have been sacrificed in this way. I (Simon) arrived in Beslan some four weeks later with a group of specialists in trauma and with a team of footballers who engaged with the surviving children in their schools and brought some much needed relief from the scenes of carnage that had engulfed the town.

As a team, we went to visit the freshly dug graves, lined up in a new cemetery that had to be specially built. Pictures of loved ones and huge bouquets of fresh flowers adorned the newly turned earth mounds where the children and adults were buried.

As we wept at the grave of one young child, a younger member of the team, whose faith was being tested by what had happened, came up to me and asked the question that was on everyone's mind, but we dared not utter: 'How can God allow this injustice to happen?'

I prayed a quick arrow prayer to ask for help, to know how to answer, and I found these words – which have stayed with me to this day – coming out of my mouth:

> I believe in a God who one day will right all the wrongs, who will bring the perpetrators to justice, who will bring freedom and new life to the victims, and who will make sense of all of this. I can't make sense of it right now, but the Bible says that there is a God who one day will untangle history and make righteous sense of it. Anyone who can do that is truly just and truly worthy of my worship and devotion.

To summarize this chapter, we lead justly not only because justice is one of the greatest themes in the Bible but also because God *is* just, God *does* justice, God is the author of justice and God calls his people to *live* justly and to *do* justice.

We live justly as a response to the grace shown to us in Jesus, we model his just leadership in our leadership – living it out in our behaviours and actions – and we anticipate a new creation where all injustices will be put right.

Reflections

1 How are you demonstrating justice through your relationships right now?
2 How is the heart of God reflected in the ways in which you lead; are you truly focused on reflecting him in all that you *say* and *do*?
3 What more might you learn about God's character that would help you to be more just?

He has shown you, O mortal, what is good.

And what does the Lord require of you?

To act justly and to love mercy

and to walk humbly with your God.

(MICAH 6.8)

2

Just me

SIMON BARRINGTON AND JUSTIN HUMPHREYS

Before we can think about what it looks like to lead justly and act justly, we want to turn our thoughts to 'What kind of *me* is needed in order to lead and act justly?' And to lead and act justly with consistency. This is at the heart of what it means to be a just leader.

Simon's story

I don't know about you, but all my attempts at leading and acting justly have been pretty inconsistent. Like many of my generation, my challenge to tackle injustice started with Live Aid on 13 July 1985. I was in my second year at university. Never before had I been exposed to the challenges of poverty and injustice in such a stark – and creative – way. Live Aid was a response to severe famine in Ethiopia – a famine that went on for three years and left an estimated 1.2 million people dead. Some 400,000 refugees fled the country, and 2.5 million people were internally displaced, while almost 200,000 children were orphaned.[1]

What followed for me were various attempts to live out Micah 6.8. Over the years this has involved serving overseas in Asia as a missionary, raising funds for charities involved in alleviating poverty globally, serving on the board of Micah Challenge in the UK, being UK CEO of one of the largest global Christian Disaster Relief organizations, being chair of a mental health charity and vice-chair of an educational charity working with those who are in danger of being excluded from school at an early age.

In all of this I have been attempting to work for justice by tackling the emerging and evident signs and symptoms of injustice. As the theologian and missiologist Chris Wright says, 'In working for justice, we address the social brokenness of human communities – with all the fractures, injustice and oppression caused by racial and gender inequality, poverty, consumerism, imperialism, greed, pride and violence.'[2]

If I'm honest, though, it's been in the midst of a middle-class lifestyle in a nice neighbourhood with good holidays, beneficial rights, access to excellent healthcare and a pension provision. That coupled with my own unconscious biases formed through years of being brought up in a mono-ethnic, mono-cultural (Welsh!) environment.

Inconsistent? Yes, extremely. Scratching at the surfaces of injustice? Absolutely. This has left me feeling that acting justly has been at the periphery rather than the heart of who I am as a leader.

More recently my heart, mind and actions have been leaning towards something much more radical and lasting. What would it take for justice to be at the heart of everything I am and everything that I do? To live out and demonstrate justice in all of my leadership interactions?

What would it take for there to be a just Simon, a just me?

Justin's story

I rarely tell the details of my own story as I'm not generally that kind of person, but over the years I have come to learn that, unquestionably, some of my experiences in life have shaped me rather than defined me. To some extent this will be true for us all. My work for the past ten-plus years has been focused on safeguarding, specifically in Christian contexts. When asked why I do this, my usual answer is that it is a fusion of my faith with my professional background and that I believe it is my calling. But the reason why this is so runs very much deeper.

I grew up in a loving Christian family – from the age of three at least. Prior to that my life had been chaotic and unstable. I had moved around the country with my mother (and sometimes father) and two siblings from here to there and back again and struggled to develop any meaningful attachments. One Christmas, soon after my second birthday, my birth mother came to a point of realizing that she couldn't carry on and signed the papers for me to be taken into the care of the local authority. I was accommodated at a residential nursery (a children's home for young children) – as the record says 'for physical and emotional recuperation'.

Despite her best efforts, my birth mother couldn't cope and had been unable to provide me with the protection, security and stability that I needed. My record states that, at the point of admission, I was recovering from an earlier period of hospitalization for bronchitis, was run-down, suffering from eczema and constant colds, underweight and withdrawn. In fact, my earliest memory was of my time spent in the security of my cot during this period in the children's home. Long story short – two years later, after numerous visits to the children's home, my adoptive parents followed God's leading and were making an application for my adoption, which was granted by the court – another of my earliest memories!

All went (relatively) smoothly from there on. That is, until a significant lifetime milestone occurred at the age of eleven. I had been excited to go to Christian summer camp. It was my chance to experience something new and my adoptive father had told me that he had gone to the camps when he was young and had arranged the same for me. This camp experience was both the best and the worst. While away, I came to know Jesus for myself. I made a lifetime commitment to follow him that summer, which was great and momentous! The trouble is, the camp chaplain who had led me to Jesus had also introduced me to something else – something uncomfortable, sinister and confusing for an eleven-year-old boy. In some ways, that confusion and consequent dilemma didn't fully kick in until years later when, as a young adult, I had to face the fact that my abuser had also been the one who introduced me to my Saviour. There was a rather large dichotomy! It is one that these days I see in the lives of many others almost every day. The privilege is mine to have some insight into their world and to do what I can to prevent others from having a similar experience.

A voice for the voiceless

Why do I tell you this now? As I mentioned, I realized some time ago that my adverse life experiences had not defined me but they had shaped me and my future to some extent. They had enabled me to understand something of injustice, the importance of restoring justice and creating safer places in families, churches, camps, charities, community groups and so on. Many would say that I am 'driven'. I would concur. That strength of perseverance in the face of what are very often tough odds is something that I have found through everything that I have been given in life. I am a firm believer that nothing is ever wasted: the good, the bad and the indifferent or confusing. God can use it all . . . and if you give him a chance, he will. For me, the call to be 'a voice for the voiceless' (Proverbs 31.8) is stronger than it has ever been. It is so significant to who I am in many ways. To be clear, it is not everything I am because that would leave no room for anything else. But there is no escaping it, my call is a very strong motivator. Every day I am learning about how God can use what I have experienced through the opportunities I have as a leader and influencer. So, how is it for you?

Image bearers

Those are our stories, but what about yours? We are all unique, all made in God's image, all image bearers. Andy Crouch, theologian and cultural commentator, has really helped us to develop our thinking on this.

> But justice is about much more than relieving suffering – it is about a vision of human flourishing . . . Even the laudable goals of economic development, political freedom, and human rights are only ultimately good when they are put in the context of something more ultimate than themselves. When we try to establish justice apart from worship of the true God, at best we will simply replace one set of false gods (and false god-players) with another. What will never be addressed by these thin, secular conceptions of justice is the heart of the biblical understanding of justice: the restoration of the human capacity to bear the image in all its fullness.[3]

That's it. How do we see the restoration of our capacity to bear the image of God in all its fullness? In Chapter 1, we saw how justice is at the heart of who God is and what God does, so the big question for us as Christian leaders is how do we become bearers of the full image of a just God in an unjust world?

Intimacy with Jesus
It starts with a searching after God in order to find our true selves. It starts with a quest for true intimacy with Jesus.

Before the COVID-19 lockdown, my wife and I (Simon) had the privilege of spending two to three weeks in a friend's cabin in the mountains of British Columbia, Canada. The scenery is nothing short of breathtaking, with crystal-clear blue water flowing into mountain-encased lakes. My experience of travelling there on a couple of occasions has been a reset of priorities and the setting of strategy for my life and business – a place where I heard clearly from God and took decisive action to set out in new directions. I was expecting the same in 2020 and went with my pen and notebook, ready to hear from God.

I was in for a shock.

As I kayaked on the wide-open St Mary's Lake, praying my heart out that God would reveal his plans and strategies for me and my business for the next two years, I clearly heard that still small voice whisper:

Simon, if only you would lay down your plans and become daily dependent on me, then we could go so much further than you can on your own. We could see so much more of my kingdom of justice and hope come – if only you would seek me first – in doing that, you will find yourself and your plans and so much more!

Not surprisingly, C. S. Lewis puts it much more brilliantly than we ever could:

Your real, new self (which is Christ's and also yours, and yours just because it is His) will not come as long as you are looking for it. It will come when you are looking for Him . . . Look for yourself, and you will find in the long run only hatred, loneliness, despair, rage, ruin, and decay. But look for Christ and you will find Him, and with Him everything else thrown in.[4]

If we are to look for justice in our own lives and leadership, we must first look for it in Christ and in our intimacy with him. Without him it is impossible to live a consistently just life, or to lead justly. When we look for him and model ourselves in his image, then we also see others made in his image – the image of a God with justice at his heart.

It is our love for Jesus, our relationship with Jesus and the knowledge that we have been graciously saved by someone from whom we deserve the exact opposite which is the starting point of being the just leaders the Bible calls us to be.

Reflecting the image

So how do we start to reflect that image, even imperfectly? We have to start with the core of our own identity and the question, 'Who am I?'

As Dallas Willard puts it:

> If I do evil, I am the kind of person who does evil; if I do good, I am the kind of person who does good (1 John 3.7–10). Actions are not impositions on who we are but are expressions of who we are. They come out of our heart and the inner realities it supervises and interacts with.[5]

Jesus puts it like this:

> A good man brings good things out of the good stored up in his heart, and an evil man brings evil things out of the evil stored up in his heart. For the mouth speaks what the heart is full of.
> (Luke 6.45)

So how do we get even close to understanding what is in our heart?

Self-intelligence

'Self-intelligence' is the ability to understand the whole of yourself – your gifts, emotions, personality, values and beliefs, and motivations – and then to act out of that understanding with increased 'emotional intelligence' and 'conversational intelligence'.

It helps us to get to an approximation of understanding what is in our hearts because it helps open up that which is unknown to us, yet seen by others, and which is known to us and we have not yet expressed.

One of the best tools for enabling self-intelligence is Johari's window (see Figure 1). The psychologists Joseph Luft and Harrington Ingham

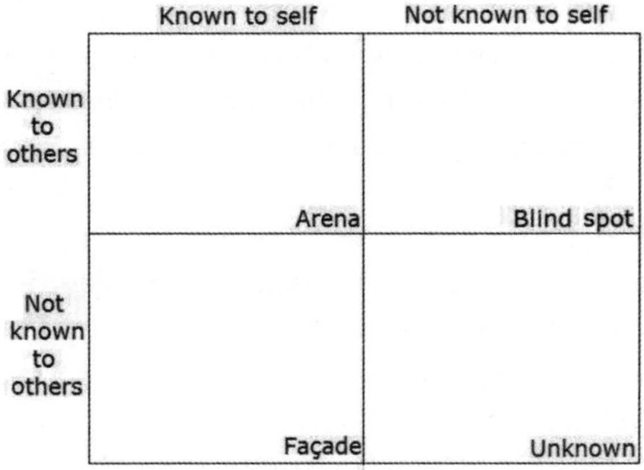

Figure 1 Johari's window

created Johari's window as a heuristic tool to enable individuals to come to a greater level of understanding of their relationship with themselves and others.

In the model, the top-left quadrant is the known self. This is the area that is public – the arena – and is known to the self and to others. It's the arena that we live in every day and is our known 'normal', but it is important to go much further than this and to look at the other three areas of the quadrant. The first of those three areas to consider is the things that others know about us and are obvious to them, but are totally unknown to us. They are our blind spots. The Achilles heel of every leader, these are the things that everyone starts talking about as soon as we leave the room, but to which we are completely oblivious.

The second of the three areas is the things that we know about ourselves, but are invisible to others. The secrets that we keep, the revelations of our true self that it needs courage and bravery to – as Brené Brown puts it – step out . . . and brave the wild.[6] This is the true me – when the façade is removed, the mask thrown off and the whole of my creative, broken, imperfect and 'glorious self' starts to emerge. These are the areas that, when revealed, allow us to bring our whole selves, vulnerably and authentically, to the table.

The final of the three areas is the most exciting: the unknown – the parts of ourselves that we don't know yet and others don't know either. The parts of our lives that we are exploring and adventuring into with others. Learning about ourselves as we try new hobbies, new foods, new activities, new cultures, new jobs, new relationships and new acts of justice.

The tool is helpful in that it can give us new windows on our hearts:

1 windows from others' perspectives, through constructive feedback;
2 windows on our inner life, as we articulate the hidden wrestles and struggles through vulnerability;
3 windows on what might be possible, as we explore new acts of justice and generosity.

However, Johari's window doesn't give us a window on our motivations – what is driving our actions and behaviours; what is motivating our heart?

What's motivating me?

Tim Keller, in his wonderful book *Generous Justice,* outlines two key motivators that he finds in Scripture for acting justly: 'joyful awe before the goodness of God's creation, and the experience of God's grace in redemption'.[7]

Here, he is naming our experience of the grace of God and the forgiveness we find in that grace as key motivators in understanding our place in acting justly, together with a right view of our place in the created order and our understanding of being made in the image of God.

If we take these as the key motivators for leading justly, then how do they match – or not – with the motivators that normally encourage us to want to pursue being a leader?

Transactional Analysis (TA) is a well-utilized tool based on psychoanalysis that was developed by Eric Berne.[8] It can be used to help leaders identify the positive motivators that drive them to want to lead in the first place. Berne identified five key drivers within what he described as the 'parent' ego state – be perfect, please others, be strong, try hard and hurry up – each of which has positive motivators, but can also result in negative messages (see Figure 2).

Berne goes on to show that there is also a shadow or dark side to each one of these motivators and drivers. When stretched, under stress or allowed to reign uncontrolled:

- **being perfect** can lead to being driven, being pedantic and being overly demanding;
- **pleasing others** can lead to inconsistency and workaholism;
- **being strong** can lead to being isolated, being a loner, a lack of vulnerability;
- **trying harder** can lead to being stressed and workaholism;
- **hurrying up** can lead to being overly focused and too demanding.

Drivers	Positive motivators	Result-in messages
Be perfect	achievement, autonomy, success, being right	Don't: make a mistake, take risks, be natural, be childlike
Please others	consideration, kindness, service	Don't: be assertive, be different, be important, say 'No'
Be strong	courage, strength, reliability	Don't: show your feelings, give in, ask for help
Try hard	persistence, patience, determination	Don't: be satisfied, relax, give up
Hurry up	speed, efficiency, responsiveness	Don't: take too long, relax, waste time

Figure 2 Transactional Analysis – the five key drivers in the parent ego state

So how can these core motivators be redeemed by applying a justice lens to them? What does it mean for each of the five drivers to be brought to their highest image-bearing form?

Being perfect becomes righteous action

At the heart of a desire to 'be perfect' is the desire for achievement, autonomy and to be right. When this is taken to the extreme, it creates drivenness and a pedantic and overly demanding nature.

When we look at this through the lens of being motivated by grace and joyful awe at the goodness of God's creation, however, then it becomes a deep desire for righteousness – for the created order to be put right and a drive towards action and achievement to do exactly that. So, our desire to be right becomes a desire to see God's righteousness worked out and our desire for achievement becomes a desire to see all humanity transformed into God's image. Even the most difficult parts of a driven, pedantic nature become graciously reshaped with a passion and hunger for right living and a graciousness when everything is not yet perfect!

Pleasing others becomes a broken heart

Core to the desire to 'please others' is a desire to show consideration for them, to act kindly towards and to serve others. When this is driven to the extreme, it becomes workaholism and a drive for affirmation from other people, which can lead to inconsistent behaviour (by trying to please everyone!)

However, God's grace and God's creation can shape this into a heart that is broken for the marginalized, the outcasts, those without any voice. Shaped in a way that increases our willingness to be assertive on their behalf and to stand out and be different, the 'please others' motivator can become a servant-hearted, margins-focused champion of justice.

Even the most challenging parts of the inconsistent and workaholic tendencies can become refined, forming a righteous backbone that is gracious and considerate to the self as well as to others.

Being strong becomes courageous challenge

Central to the motivator to 'be strong' are the positive attributes of courage, reliability and strength. Yet the extremes can be ugly, taking the forms of isolation, loneliness and hiding vulnerabilities behind a mask.

Having a justice-shaped heart, though, can transform these extreme negative attributes so that, instead, being strong manifests as speaking out on the most difficult subjects, keeping going for the long term, even when everyone else gives up, and allowing the grace of God to permeate deep inside to reveal the flawed and yet awesome (or as our friend Patrick Regan says 'flawsome'[9]) aspects of that person's nature.

26

Even the most challenging parts of the 'stiff upper lip' characteristics of the 'be strong' motivator can be melted into a soft-hearted, but strong backbone personality who engages relationally with others to fight against some of the most difficult issues, such as female genital mutilation (FGM), sexual abuse and, indeed, loneliness and social isolation itself.

Trying harder becomes determined struggle

Those whose core motivation is to 'try harder' can often end up getting stressed and suffering burnout. They can't give themselves a moment to relax and feel that they just have to keep on going and going and going, often to the detriment of their own health.

However, the underlying characteristics of persistence – never giving up, a determination to tackle the hard stuff and perseverance, even when the going gets tough – are godly, justice-centred characteristics.

When focused on the most marginalized in society and on the toughest, hardest to crack, most demanding situations that require generational change – such as climate justice and anti-human trafficking campaigns – the sheer dogged nature of people who are willing to push through is inspiring and regenerative.

Stress and workaholism – the marks of the 'try harder' motivation when pushed to the limits – are revolutionized by the grace of God and awe at his created order. In God, we find our rightful place and the knowledge of our limitations. In God, we receive undeserved mercy that assures us it doesn't all depend on us and, ultimately, what we desire most – the conquering of death and relationship with God – is only possible because he acted first. Liberated 'try harders' become determined strugglers in partnership with God for the victory over unfairness that is God's alone.

Hurrying up becomes a holy antagonist

'Hurry ups' can never slow down. They are naturally impatient to see change, anxious for progress and drive for efficiency. They want immediate results, immediate responses and even waiting for their porridge to heat in the microwave is intolerable for them.

Freedom for those with the 'hurry up' motivator at their core comes as the grace of God brings them patience to go at the speed that God sets, a willingness to push through when delays come, alongside a holy antagonism to see progress and results.

When their attention is drawn to the chasm in parity between the poorest and the richest, the disadvantage faced by women and girls in education, the impact of climate change, then they can't wait to get started, can't wait to start agitating and look for the quickest wins, the biggest changes and the most effective solutions.

Will you allow the grace of God to break your heart?

Bob Pierce, the founder of both World Vision and Samaritan's Purse – two of the largest Christian international relief organizations in the world, had a simple motto: 'Let my heart be broken by the things that break the heart of God.'[10]

Will you pray that audacious, dangerous, radical prayer and allow the grace of the Lord Jesus and the joyful awe of your place in God's creation to sweep over your heart and life and radicalize and redeem your natural leadership motivations for God's glory?

The rocky road

'I love cake! Why couldn't God give me a ministry about cake?'

My friend and colleague Dr Lisa Oakley, with whom I (Justin) co-authored my last book, regularly shares the thoughts she sometimes has of wishing God had given her an easier mission or ministry. She loves cake and all things cake-related – which is all very nice, after all one could study and sample cake until the day we die. But God gave her a call to pursue the issue of abuse in the Church – and specifically the issue of spiritual abuse. It is genuinely heartbreaking territory. In that call and her obedience to it, she has become, without question, one of the world's foremost experts on the subject.

Why is it that God pulls us towards the very things that we are frustrated by or feel a deep sense of discomfort about? Why is it that God chooses to use our deepest regrets, most painful experiences, motivations and hardest life lessons for his kingdom? It's a brave and bold person who rejects the apparent call of God in pursuit of comfortable things as a way to avoid the tough stuff. While this is undoubtedly a most difficult call, there is something extraordinary to be achieved through the life of the willing disciple who knows this and, despite the rocky road (no pun intended) ahead, sticks with the journey and sacrifices herself for the greater good. Just for the record, Lisa knows well that she is pursuing the right course. It just helps occasionally not to take yourself too seriously and laugh about what could have been.

In being willing to travel this journey, Lisa's selfless ability to give herself away and be led by God in pursuit of a difficult cause has created just the right environment in which others have been able to come alongside, to collaborate, to endeavour together to change the Church and society for good. She is a leader with justice at her core, bearing the image of God and has allowed her motivations and character to be shaped after the heart of God.

Reflections

1 What experiences have you had that challenged your concept of justice and motivated you to be more mindful of the injustice experienced by others?
2 How does your understanding of your whole self – your gifts, emotions, personality, values, beliefs and motivations – have an impact on the way in which you lead?
3 Have you been fully open to the possibility that God might want to use your brokenness to lead you into a deeper understanding of his love for others? DLCH

I am because we are.

MOTTO OF UBUNTU THEOLOGY

3

Just us

JUSTIN HUMPHREYS AND SIMON BARRINGTON

Ubuntu

Having established what kind of 'me' it takes to lead justly, and with all this focus on ourselves and our individual motivations, it is important now to move on and focus on what impact this has on others.

We are never isolated and alone, never acting with justice in separation from others. This is a key idea that exists throughout our thinking about justice and leadership in this book – it's all about relationship.

South African Anglican bishop Desmond Tutu's Christian take on the African ubuntu philosophy is helpful in this respect, in that it recognizes the humanity of people through their relationships with others. Drawing from his Christian faith, Tutu theologizes ubuntu by utilizing a model in which human dignity and identity are drawn from the image of a relational God. We are called to be relational because God is relational. The motto of ubuntu theology is 'I am because we are'. Therefore, in seeking a 'just me' I must also seek after a 'just you' and a 'just us', because we are all made in the image of a 'just God'.

Me, you and the formation of us

As discussed in the last chapter, it is important for us to be clear about the relationship between 'me', 'you' and the formation of 'us' when considering just leadership. As we have both explored, the need to understand 'me' is critical, but knowing what is reasonable to expect of others in our pursuit of justice is just as important.

When my (Justin) father died, one of the treasures that he left behind was his battered and worn box set of Tolkien's *The Lord of the Rings* trilogy. The box is falling apart and the spines are so split that you can barely read the titles of each book, but within those tattered pages, the story carries so much depth of meaning and creativity.

There are so many memorable moments, but one that stands out is one of the discussions between Frodo Baggins (the main character) and Samwise Gamgee (his best friend and companion) on one of the pages that falls out of my dad's old book when opened. On the epic journey to return the 'one ring' to the fires of Mount Doom where it was originally forged, at the foot of the mountain, Frodo becomes desperately tired: both physically and mentally. The metaphorical weight of the mission that he had taken on was becoming too much, as were the physical demands and the recognition of the evil forces that he was battling. Frodo *literally* owned and wore his purpose (the ring) and he felt the weight of responsibility that it brought. Then comes this beautiful encouragement from Samwise to Frodo: 'Come, Mr Frodo, I can't carry it for you, but I can carry you and it as well!'[1]

Samwise knew that he could not hold the ring. It was not his responsibility and he would probably not have been able to withstand its dark power even if he thought he should hold it. But he was able to assist his friend to carry that burden and in just being there alongside him, that was what he did. You might even say that just being there was his only role in the entire story. It was the strength of that collaboration, faithfulness and unswerving support that made the whole journey possible. Different roles, different gifts and different perspectives, but togetherness was the result. Both Frodo and Samwise understood that just 'me' wasn't enough for either of them. What they needed was 'us'. An 'us' that was unified in purpose and mission.

So the question might be to you as a leader: have you found that person or those people who might support you in your endeavours? Can you ask them for what you need of them and whether they might be prepared to join you? You might even feel able to say: I need you, just you!

The crazy mirror

Once you fully appreciate the need to have a common purpose with those around you, the next question is what exactly do you need in your relationship with them? Sometimes, when we are determined to press forward to see change or achieve something significant, we can unwittingly forget to even ask the question. There might even be times when we take the support of others for granted, or worse still reject it completely (as Frodo did with Sam at times throughout their epic adventure).

When all is said and done, the just leader needs a just you (or multiple just yous). But what does this mean? At times, we need to stand back and take some time to hold the mirror up to ourselves and take a long hard look at what we see. Do we see in ourselves what we hope to see in others? And is the commonality that we find with those around us in the areas of our character and purpose both healthy and just? One of my favourite quotes through much reading on the subject of leadership is by Stephen Covey, who says:

> If the only vision we have of ourselves comes from the social mirror – from the current social paradigm and the opinions, perceptions and paradigms of the people around us – our view of ourselves is like the reflection in the crazy mirror room at the carnival.[2]

We have to question what and who we are surrounded by and what motivates us to make the relational connections that we have. Being swayed by the latest trends, platitudes and adoration of others is a dangerous place to be. When these influences are driven by the incredibly powerful need for belonging, van der Hart and Waller suggest that we find the 'sociometer' can take us off course and leave us with an inaccurate view of ourselves and the world around us.[3] So, in identifying what 'just me' looks like, we can then reach beyond ourselves and hope to find a 'just you' to keep us grounded, motivated, supported and challenged.

Giving yourself away

I'm both intrigued and challenged by this notion of what it means to give yourself away in pursuit of a common purpose. Not just in terms of who we might give ourselves to, but how to achieve this in a balanced way that is ultimately productive for all concerned and that builds strong healthy relationships.

In recent years, I have had the benefit and privilege of receiving executive coaching in my workplace. This has been an immensely positive exercise that has assisted me to explore a range of ideas, struggles and realities about leadership in the Christian charity sector. It was in one such session with my coach that I was faced with a hard question. I had expressed the sense of guilt and inadequacy I felt by taking time out of the relentless busyness of the workplace to spend on developing myself and my leadership. 'Why do you struggle?' I was asked. 'What makes you feel that sense of guilt?' I had to face the fact that I felt a dilemma caused by that lying, nagging voice of shame and criticism, which was ultimately neither helpful for me nor anyone else. As Swann puts it: 'Most powerful of all is our own interior voice that demands everything and fears that to give time to self is to take it away from others.'[4]

This realization that it was actually healthier to invest time in myself was not new. I had just chosen to ignore its truth and carry on as I always had. The reality is that in denying my own development, I was in fact denying my colleagues and the wider organizational mission the benefit of my learning. As we have already said, and will say again, the just leader has difficult territory to navigate, both in their commitment to acting justly and in achieving justice for others. We owe it to ourselves to ensure we are equipped, empowered and encouraged in every way possible to do this well. Today, the need for others alongside you might be yours. Tomorrow it may be your turn to get alongside somebody else.

I don't know about you, but there is one phrase that I keep hearing over and over again these days. To be frank, I can't stand it because I think it is over-used and has become one of those trendy phrases used in too many circles and it begins to lose any truth or power it might have carried:

'Be the best version of yourself.'

What does that even mean? How many versions of me are available? Maybe I'm being unfair. Maybe the potential power is lost when it is applied in questionable or shallow contexts. Let's give it the benefit of exploration in this context for a moment. Can it be applied to this idea of giving yourself away? I think it probably can. If we aspire to high standards and seek to give the very best, then perhaps we have to spend time investing in our own growth before we have the best to give to others.

There – I've gone and done it and made use of something I have previously criticized. As much as it may seem counter-intuitive, understanding that our relational connectedness and synergy with others (as we will explore further in later chapters) is where the power to create change is best used and can make all the difference.

Generous collaboration

There is no doubt that justice requires partnership. There are too many issues, too many barriers to be broken down and systems to be challenged, to think that we can do this alone – even with the highest levels of individual sacrifice and service.

It's one thing to include individuals in co-creation of the future but collaborating across organizations can be fraught with difficulty. Our individual agendas (however well meaning) once they have become enveloped in the cloak of organizational structures can be the most intractable to shake. It takes a leader with courage and persistence and a determined generosity to break through systems, processes, structures and mindsets to find a better way.

In our research on millennials, published in *Leading – the Millennial Way* in 2019, Rachel Luetchford and I (Simon) noted that there is a significant generational shift towards greater levels of collaboration, born out of a larger world-view formed by greater access to information and knowledge.[5] This mindset starts to ask the proactive question: 'Why aren't we collaborating to solve the world's largest problems?' This is a significant shift from the suggestion, 'Why don't we collaborate?'

As leaders we need a more generous model of collaboration towards justice, one that is rooted in Scripture, where I see four key principles:

1 a sharing in a common cause (Philippians 1.5, 4.3, 15);
2 a sharing of spiritual and practical gifts (1 Corinthians 12.7; Ephesians 4.11–13);
3 a sharing in suffering (1 Corinthians 12.26; 2 Corinthians 1.7; Philippians 3.10);
4 a sharing in material resources (Romans 15.24–29; 2 Corinthians 8.1–15; 9.1–5).

The missiologist Charles Van Engen proposes the following theological approach to new partnerships based on a study of Ephesians 4.1—5.2. A model that we can easily apply to new justice-focused partnerships, understanding the pursuit of justice as a fundamental part of joining in with the Missio Dei

> . . . because the church's oneness is centered in Jesus Christ (the motivation for mission), Christians are called to partner together for world evangelization, serving one another in love and humility (the agency of mission) as they participate in Christ's mission, offering to one another the unique gifts given by the Holy Spirit to their various regional and global organizations and churches (the means of mission), so that they may equip the saints for the work of ministry until they all together grow up into the measure of the stature of the fullness of Christ (the goals of mission partnerships).[6]

Here we can start to see a way forwards towards a generous inclusivity as we collaboratively seek a transformative justice in society.

It starts with a generously orthodox focus on our oneness in Jesus Christ and the inclusivity that flows from that. It moves towards a genuine desire to serve and love one another out of humility, from which springs a common desire to join in with Christ's mission to bring justice and wholeness. It is only then that we offer our unique gifts and experiences to one another with a desire to sacrifice for the greater or common good.

That's where it starts getting tricky though. In Chapter 6 we talk about the need for voices from outside us to keep our motivations and egos in their right place. My genuine experience is that individually we desire this practice of sacrifice for the greater good, but organizationally we have yet to learn how to do that well.

I wonder what the effect would be if we set our goal not on the completion of individual justice projects but, rather, on the desire that we are all equipped for the work of justice and we all together grow up into the measure of the stature of the fullness of Christ. That's a great one to have on your organization's data dashboard!

Sacrificing for the greater good?

Choosing to take on the fight for justice and surrounding yourself with others who share that same commitment is at the heart of the Bible. But how do we do that in a way that doesn't leave us feeling like we are burnt-out and wrung-out with little left to give?

Committing ourselves to this singular pursuit of justice (in whatever form that takes) requires self-sacrifice, which is a powerful thing and creates the space for greater levels of collaboration and deeper relationships.

Self-sacrifice is actually very closely tied to the concept of justice, dilemmas and ethically or morally driven decision-making.[7] It's right there in the opening statement of this chapter: I am because we are. We won't achieve the 'we are' without self-sacrifice – as we saw above.

What and who will you give yourself away for? We're all in this fight for justice together.

Reflections

1 Have you fully appreciated that God's plan is that we do things together rather than on our own and that *just leadership* requires the most skilful application of this to fully succeed?
2 Who have you surrounded yourself with? Do they truly support you to live out and lead in a justice-focused way?
3 How good are you at offering your unique gifts and experiences to others with a desire to sacrifice yourself for the greater or common good?

Part 2

JUST LEADERSHIP

Introduction to Part 2

We have already seen how *just leaders* need a theology of justice with God at the centre, how we need a greater understanding of who we are – our identity – and how we need to give ourselves away in the pursuit of a common cause by creating an environment in which others can join in.

In Part 2 we turn our attention to some really practical skills and attributes that are the hallmarks of a leader who 'does justice' and who restores relationships with others and with creation. Here we are not concerned about the just causes you will fight for, but your heart, your approach and your posture – in other words, putting integrity and justice at the heart of the way that you lead.

What does this look like in practice for those who are in leadership?

How can we be sure that the foundations we build will lead to our actions aligning with our beliefs and our identity? In other words, how can we act authentically and with integrity? It is to these questions that we now turn. Within this largest section of the book, we have attempted to provide additional focus by dividing it into the following subsections.

1 **Just leadership: foundations (Chapters 4—7)** Foundational to the heart of a just leader are the attributes of speaking up, hearing diverse voices and being willing to walk the journey with those suffering injustice.
2 **Just leadership: posture (Chapters 8—11)** Core leadership postures for a just leader include coming close to injustice, generosity, managing power and being courageous.
3 **Just leadership: action (Chapters 12—15)** How do just leaders act – with transparency, accountability, a passion for change and a willingness to tackle conflict.

JUST LEADERSHIP: FOUNDATIONS

Speak out on behalf of the voiceless, and for the rights of all who are vulnerable.

Speak out in order to judge with righteousness and to defend the needy and the poor.

(PROVERBS 31.8–9, CEB)

4

Speaking up

JUSTIN HUMPHREYS

When we are given a platform, whether literally or metaphorically, we are also given great responsibility to use it well. So here's a question straight off the bat . . . When you step on to your platform, what is the first thing that comes to your mind? Is it how *you* look, how *you* feel, how *you* might come across, or is it about how you might hold your influence humbly and demonstrate justice for *others* through your words and actions?

If we're honest, the first three are all probably legitimate thoughts that we have all had at some stage. Let's face it, none of us likes to look or feel foolish or unprepared, least of all when we are in front of others leading the way. The challenge here is not to stop being human, but to consider something deeper about how we use the positions of influence that we have for the good of others. When faced with challenges, what is your first reaction – where do you go instinctively? We've heard it said so many times that we show the most of ourselves and our character when we are under pressure or facing challenging circumstances. Again, if we're honest, putting the needs of others before our own is perhaps not always something that comes naturally or instinctively.

Every person for themselves!

I recall the story that Hayley, my wife, has repeated periodically throughout our twenty-seven years of marriage. It makes me cringe every time she retells it. She recounts an occasion when, prior to being married, we were on a night out at the infamous 'The Station' pub in our home town with some friends (most of whom were from our church young adults group, if I remember correctly). During the course of the evening, some other patrons of the establishment (not our group) got a bit rowdy and a fight broke out on the tables next to us. Before we knew what was going on, tables and chairs started to fly. In that split moment, when drinks are being spilled and there is little opportunity to think, swift eye contact is required with few words to execute a safe exit plan. Basically, let's get out of here – fast!

The way Hayley remembers and recounts the story is that my instinctive reaction was 'every person for themselves . . . run', leaving her to make her own way away from the hostile crowd behind me. Of course, I do not remember things in quite the same way, although clarity is beginning to fade somewhat after almost thirty years!

Regardless, the illustration makes a good point. Could I have taken more time to ensure the safety of others before making my way out of the building? The answer is obvious – yes, it would seem that I could. Whatever my thoughts and actions were at that time, they did not give Hayley the confidence that I had her best interests at heart and above my own. That's a painful reflection, if I'm honest. Maybe I have just fooled myself about this for all these years when protesting what I believed to be a skewed recollection of events. Maybe I just wasn't attentive enough. What would it have taken for this story to have looked more like a tale of somebody who truly had justice and the protection of others at the forefront of his mind? Or at the very least somebody who was prepared to speak up in order to assist others?

A clue to this might be found in the passage of Scripture at the start of this chapter (Proverbs 31.8–9). This verse and those that surround it provide a wonderful picture of a life lesson taught to a king by his mother. They point as much towards those things that appear to have become customary at the time as to those attitudes and behaviours which would represent a leadership change from that norm. So who was this king and what is so significant about this passage?

A mother's lesson

First, when I reflect on this passage, I am struck by the fact that it details the words of a king (Lemuel), based on what he had been taught by his mother (Proverbs 31.1). This surely could not just have been a casual conversation between them. It was something learned, something so profound which had such an impact on this king that he felt the need to repeat it, commit it to writing and offer it as a blueprint for his leadership and the leadership of others. Within this, I see something that speaks to the very heart of leadership in our culture today.

According to research undertaken into the prevalence of female executive leaders across the 193 member states of the United Nations, the number of female leaders has never been more than 10 per cent of all leaders at any point since 1960.[1] This troubles me greatly, as I have seen that the leadership landscape has been deprived of the female perspective for too long. We have to accept that a different perspective is often brought by women in leadership, often one that is more compassionate. When we are thinking about issues of justice and injustice, this perspective is desperately needed. I see that need all the time in the many churches and organizations that I work alongside through the difficulties caused by abusive, coercive and controlling leaders and the cultures they maintain. Incidentally, these types of leaders are rarely ever women.

It's not a stretch to think that King Lemuel's mother was herself a queen at some stage, or at least someone of great influence in the royal courts of the day. Maybe, even at the time of teaching her son this crucial life lesson, he may not yet have been king and she would have been exercising her responsibility to prepare him well for what he was about to step into as a person of power and influence. Where are those female leaders in our world today? It is an important question that we need to ask ourselves. There may be countless potential explanations for this. At its deepest level, we may still be witnessing the perpetuation of the horrific ploy of the enemy to rid the world of women by stealth, therefore dismantling the equilibrium of life as God intended it. Reflecting on the words in Genesis 3.15, this argument is made passionately by Lisa Bevere in her exploration of gendercide and infanticide established as a strategy from the earliest times:

Enmity is deep-rooted hatred and irreconcilable hostility. This describes a breach so profound that with each passing generation, Satan's hostility and hatred deepen as he runs out of time and the urgency increases. Never has his attack against women and children been more wicked, obvious, and widespread.[2]

Maybe you think this is a stretch too far? But the question still remains – why are there still so many organizations and groups that find it so hard to acknowledge the invaluable perspective brought by women? Why are there so many of those organizations that refuse to address the issue of women being absent in their leadership positions? In some respects, I have been privileged to work in the social work profession that has bucked this trend to a degree. An embedded understanding of the importance of equality and women's rights is intrinsic to the ethos of social work. It is of such high importance that it finds focus within the United Nations Sustainable Development Goals towards building gender-equitable societies.[3]

I am also privileged to be joint CEO of a national charity whose senior leadership team of eight is split 50/50 between men and women. Although I couldn't say hand-on-heart that we orchestrated this completely, a recognition of the need to establish gender equality within this group has certainly influenced our recruitment choices. We are all the better and more balanced for those choices too!

This is not the place to attempt to do real justice to this important issue as it will most definitely fall way short of the exploration it deserves. The point I make here is that this issue of gender inequality within leadership is one that is likely responsible for many failings in global leadership in recent times. Achieving an appropriate gender balance in our leadership teams is one of the essential ingredients for a justice-focused culture and way of working. If we do not champion the role of women in leadership, we will deny ourselves the privilege of hearing their voice: a voice that we desperately need to bring insight and balance in our collective efforts to speak out and advocate for the rights of others in society.

Believe me, I have seen the different ways in which organizations (even those that purport to be justice-focused) have made difficult situations so much more difficult, leaving a distinct impression that had they engaged their female leaders more proactively, the situation would have been handled so much better. Anecdotally, in some organizations I am aware of, the very lack of female leaders on senior leadership teams

48

could be seen as one of the key factors in those organizations finding themselves in a bit of a mess. This is particularly the case when looking at managing HR-related matters that require a keen focus on 'soft systems' approaches.[4] In fact, these 'softer' issues are becoming the heart of learning organizations and need to be at the core of every leader's thinking and not just HR issues.

Standing on the threshold of words into action

The second point of reflection on this passage in Proverbs is that it is a call to action. In a way, the first half of the passage (v. 8) that I have highlighted at that start of the chapter is the precursor to the second half (v. 9). If you like, the boldness and preparedness to speak out is where we start, but it is as a means to be active to effect change and see justice worked out, especially for those who have no voice, or who are disadvantaged or oppressed in some way. This requires courage (which we will explore later in Chapter 11).

How many times in your life have you been in a situation where you had that horrid inner battle going on where you have fought with yourself about whether or not to stand up and speak out about something? You know, that time when your heart was pounding so much that you thought it would explode inside your chest, yet the more you tried to ignore it, the heavier your heart would pound. You know that you have to say something! I'm not talking about glossophobia as such, which describes what is often referred to as 'stage fright' or 'performance anxiety'. I'm talking about those situations when your experiences, values, beliefs, attitudes and passions collide to the point that the adrenalin rushing round your body is giving you a sign that you may be about to contribute something really important to what's going on around you.

This is often the doorway between who you are and what you are here for. In other words, for those of us that choose to be filled and guided by the Holy Spirit, these times can be those that God uses for his glory and the benefit of others. The element of fear that we may be encountering in that heart-pumping moment is likely to be all those negative, often irrational voices that would say to us 'you're no good' or 'that would be a crazy thing to say'. Worse still that sense of 'imposter syndrome' that often comes calling – believe me, I've heard that voice many times! Whether we attribute those voices to the enemy or not, getting past these and opening the door is where we begin and often start to see the greatest impact. For those of you who find the concept of opening that door a nerve-wracking prospect, you might be encouraged by the words of Billy Graham: 'When we come to the end of ourselves, we come to the beginning of God'.

I understand that Billy Graham spoke these words in the context of the power of prayer. However, they are no less true in this context. If you're reading this book, the chances are that you have a justice mindset already, or at least are interested enough to discover what we might mean by *just leadership*. So I imagine it's likely that one of the things that is going to bring you to standing on the threshold of speaking out is your sense of justice. What a beautiful place to be standing! Can you visualize what God might be about to do through you?

Parrhesiastes – speaking truth to power

Returning to the passage from Proverbs, what do we learn about the purpose of speaking out? Being a king, it is fair to assume that Lemuel had power, influence and wealth. The incredible thing about this short passage is that amid all the things that he might have achieved as king, he chose to focus his resources and attentions – at least in part – on actions that would benefit others. In this case, those who have no voice of their own (figuratively), those who were seen to be vulnerable and those who were poor and needy.

If we were to question for a moment what it is that renders people voiceless, or vulnerable or disadvantaged, it almost always boils down to inequality, imbalance or oppression of some kind. A person or system behaving in a way that creates or perpetuates that situation for another person or group. Speaking out against such situations is what King Lemuel appears to be committing to as a matter of great importance. What an amazing picture of speaking truth to power. In his writings and lectures, Foucault describes the Greek origin and meaning of this act in his understanding of parrhesiastes and how they speak out:

To my mind, the parrhesiastes says what is true because he knows that it is true; and he knows that it is true because it is really true. The parrhesiastes is not only sincere and says what is his opinion, but his opinion is also the truth. He says what he knows to be true . . . there is always an exact coincidence between belief and truth.[5]

Challenging those within power structures and authorities, who may be creating oppression or disadvantage, with objectivity, compassion and truth, is a privilege, but sometimes not without consequences. Throughout the Bible, and particularly the Old Testament, we read of the prophets who brought words of challenge to the people. This often put them on the outside, isolated and sometimes rejected completely. Ultimately, isn't this what we see in the life of Jesus himself? If we were to take a modern-day example of this, we could learn much from the story of Rachael Denhollander, who spoke out about years of abuse by Larry Nassar, the USA gymnastics team doctor. In her account given to the New York Times, she describes the impact of advocating on behalf of the countless other victims of Nassar:

I lost my church. I lost my closest friends as a result of advocating for survivors who had been victimized by similar institutional failures in my own community. I lost every shred of privacy.[6]

A 'calling' to speak out

This was an exceptional account of courage and parrhesia that has inspired many around the world. But hearing this, we might still say, 'is it any wonder we have only a limited number of leaders who are prepared to speak out?' Nobody said that speaking out would ever be easy. It is clear in this account and many others that there can be a price to pay. But isn't it still the right thing to do? Isn't what King Lemuel was talking about sufficient to give us a mandate to speak out?

I hold the view that we are all 'called' to understand and practise justice in society, but there are also those who are additionally 'called' to a specific ministry of justice. For these people, speaking out has become an integral and critical aspect of their work and ministry. For them, a choice has been made to accept the pain in the journey and the reality that this will not often afford them any wins in the popularity stakes. Why is this so? Because the necessity of speaking out is based on a need to change something that has been to something that could be: change in oppressive power structures; change in economic and social poverty and disadvantage; change in climate-damaging activities, or change in harmful and abusive behaviours.

Who will 'stay the course' with you?

I believe, therefore, that we all have a clear mandate that comes from the heart of Scripture to speak out on behalf of others. Some of us will know people for whom this is a specific response to a call: a mandate, motivation and mission in life.[7] Where we know such people, we must get alongside them and pray for them. Seek them out and let them know that you are praying. Often, they may not be able to share the specifics of what they are working on or going through, but I can tell you that just the knowledge that you are praying and cheering them on is sustaining in itself!

Dr Lisa Oakley (my co-author of *Escaping the Maze of Spiritual Abuse*[8]) regularly sends me a text or message out of the blue just to say, 'I'm praying for you and whatever you're doing today' or something similar. I cannot tell you what this means in the cut and thrust of some of the most challenging work I have ever encountered. Another good friend of mine, Dr Wess Stafford (Emeritus President of Compassion International) once said to me, 'If you are doing this kind of work, it is as if you have a huge target on your chest for the enemy to fire at. You must be ready and prepared for this.'

Ensuring that those pursuing a calling to speak out for others in this way have ready access to personal and pastoral support is essential to avoiding emotional, mental or spiritual exhaustion and assisting their long-term success. If you are that person and you do not have those support mechanisms in place already, I would strongly encourage you to seek them out. Identifying a small group of people who you trust to stay the course with you, hold you to account, check-in with you one-to-one and offer prayer will be a life-saver to many of you.

When the silence is deafening

To conclude this chapter, I want to leave you with one very important aspect of speaking up. That is, what happens when nobody takes it on themselves to lend their voices to others in need. The silence around issues of abuse and other similar injustices can be deafening. All too often, the victims and survivors are left to be the only ones speaking for themselves. When this happens, it is an appalling example of how they can be re-abused and, for some, where they feel as though they are reliving the very abuse that they have sought to bring into the light. In certain cases, this literally has left them penniless and destitute.

In recent times we have seen the #MeToo movement give life and voice to those who have been forced into silence for decades following sexual harassment in the workplace, rape, sexual assault and abuses of other kinds. Breaking the silence on issues of abuse and harassment requires our voices. As much as the #MeToo movement has brought the magnitude of such matters into the public consciousness, it cannot be left there with the only people speaking out being those that have already suffered. We must lend our voices too.

In case there was any doubt or confusion, it is not just the worlds of celebrity, music, film and the arts that suffer from such injustices. The corporate, charity and Church worlds have provided a foothold for such acts too. Indeed, raising attention to 'sector-specific' examples by using the hashtag has seen the use of #ChurchToo as a sad addition, highlighting the fact that no aspect of society seems to be excluded from this pandemic of gender-based violence and injustice.

Let's not fool ourselves that 'this doesn't happen here'. Let's not be blinkered to the widespread and varying nature of these abuses and injustices either. Sexual, physical, emotional, psychological and spiritual abuses of all kinds occur everywhere. The question we need to ask ourselves as leaders is what are we going to do about it? Are you prepared to spend the time understanding the issues by being close to those who have suffered (as we explore in Chapter 6) and speaking out? Are you then prepared to cross the threshold, open the door and move to action? If the answer to these questions is yes, then you have just accepted a mission to walk the path of justice!

Reflections

1 Where might the silence be deafening, where God is calling you to speak out?
2 Can you visualize what God might want to do through you as you stand on the threshold of speaking out?
3 How can you support and encourage those whom God has called to speak truth to power?

If I only had a voice

That would speak for me with love

If we only had a choice

We would rise against injustice

I don't care how much you know

Till I know how much you care

And there's only so much load

That I'm capable of bearing

Hear my voice

Be my justice.

SOMEBODY PLEASE HEAR MY VOICE — ONE VOICE
COLLECTIVE[1]

5

Hearing the voices from the outside

SIMON BARRINGTON

> The ear of the leader must ring with the voices of the people.
> Woodrow Wilson[2]

Hearing different voices from our own

Being willing to listen to a wide variety of voices and hear different perspectives, while being secure in our own sense of identity, is a mark of justice-based leadership. It involves setting aside our own prejudices and entering into the other's world. M. Scott Peck, the American psychiatrist and author of *The Road Less Travelled*, puts it extremely well:

> An essential part of true listening is the discipline of bracketing, the temporary giving up or setting aside of one's own prejudices, frames of reference and desires so as to experience as far as possible the speaker's world from the inside, stepping inside his or her shoes. This unification of speaker and listener is actually an extension and enlargement of ourselves, and new knowledge is always gained from this.[3]

This kind of listening – fully accepting the other so that they can be truly themselves – is at the heart of a justice-based leader. The willingness to step inside someone else's shoes and see the world through a different lens. To hear a different voice. The willingness to be shocked, to be taken aback, to relearn and to think the once unimaginable requires a security of identity and a deep understanding of our own core.

57

We are so used to bringing our own lenses to the way that we view the world – lenses that have been shaped by our cultural upbringing, our parents, our schooling and the television and YouTube videos we have watched – that it often takes us by surprise that other people can see things SO differently.

Take reading the Bible, for instance . . .

Reading the Bible from a different angle

Let's take Exodus 20.8–10:

> Remember the Sabbath day by keeping it holy. Six days you shall labour and do all your work, but the seventh day is a sabbath to the Lord your God. On it you shall not do any work, neither you, nor your son or daughter, nor your male or female servant, nor your animals, nor any foreigner residing in your towns.

When we read this from the position of privilege and employment, we are likely to focus on helping people see the need to rest, to take a day off, to slow down and to spend time with our families because that is what God did – he rested on the seventh day. We read the passage from the privilege of being employed. As the author of *Reading the Bible from the Margins*, Miguel A. De La Torre, explains:

> We are blinded to the fact that sections of our society lack opportunities for employment due to their race, ethnicity, gender or class. By imposing upon the text our assumption of class privilege we are oblivious to the first part of the text 'Six days you shall labour'.[4]

How would you, therefore, prepare a sermon for a community where a factory has just been shut down or where there are high levels of unemployment and people are on their five-hundredth job application and have yet to get an interview?

When we read the Bible from the margins and listen to it and hear other voices, we realize that our economy is not set up to enable a large percentage of the population to be able to keep God's commandment to work for six days. What should we do to challenge this situation?

Surely that is the work of a justice-based leader who can listen to and hear other voices. A justice-based leader who is not so focused on reading the world through her own lens that she is not able to see the world through other people's eyes. It is also the work of a justice-based leader to read the Scriptures through the lens of those who are most marginalized in society. Sometimes this can have an impact on a whole nation.

When I was 21, I had the privilege of living in Taiwan for a year. Taiwan was and is in a struggle for its own identity. In 1945, following the end of the Second World War, the nationalist government of mainland China, led by the Kuomintang (KMT), invaded and took control of Taiwan. In 1949, after losing control of mainland China in the Chinese Civil War, the mainland China government under the KMT withdrew to Taiwan and Chiang Kai-Shek declared martial law. The KMT ruled Taiwan as a single-party state for forty years, until democratic reforms in the 1980s, which led to the first ever direct presidential election in 1996.

I lived in Taiwan during the indigenous Taiwanese people's struggle to determine for themselves the future of their country and to experience the liberation and freedoms that they once knew. The Presbyterian Church of Taiwan (PCT) was in the middle of that huge struggle and was highly influential in its voice on behalf of the Taiwanese people. They read the Bible in ways that I had never imagined.

From 1971 on, the PCT remained an insistent and consistent voice for human rights and democracy. Calling for Taiwan to become 'a new and independent nation', it also formulated an inclusive vision of a nation encompassing all the people groups in Taiwan, 'a new and independent country' achieved through non-violent struggle based on 'love and suffering'. This role derived from its strong contemporary Calvinist faith and self-identity of the Church as both 'universal and rooted in this land'.

The Israelites' struggle for freedom from Egypt took on a whole new perspective for the people of Taiwan. The calls to 'set my people free' resonated deeply in their souls, as did the announcement by Jesus as he inaugurated his ministry that he had come to 'set the captives free'. The PCT's campaign for justice was a campaign to see kingdom liberties for their people in the here and now.

Back in the 1970s and 1980s, Liberation Theology had a very bad name among evangelicals. However, thanks to the work of John Stott,

Chris Wright and the Lausanne Movement, leaders who listened to the struggles and challenges of their global neighbours were able to declare that Christians should share God's 'concern for justice and reconciliation throughout human society and for the liberation of men and women from every kind of oppression'.[5]

As John Coffey so helpfully states in his Cambridge Paper, 'To release the oppressed: Reclaiming a biblical theology of liberation':

> The Bible reveals a God who hears the cries of the oppressed and loves to bring deliverance. The mission of God sets an agenda for the Church. In our preaching, prayer and worship we need to recover an integrated vision of the gospel as a message of liberation 'from every kind of oppression'. Church should not be a cosy retreat from the world, an insulated spiritual bubble containing privatised piety. Instead, churches ought to pray for the spiritual and material needs of the world and educate and empower their members to tackle injustice.

This willingness to engage with the Bible in a way that reads it through the eyes of people who have and are suffering from oppression and injustice is a necessity for any justice-based leader.

I was once part of a global gathering of Christian leaders in the USA. We were a group that met regularly and that had the tendency to look at the world through a particular world-view. My Irish colleague felt this discomfort most acutely and was always laughing about the narrow perspective we were taking.

At one annual get-together, he produced a special gift for us all. A pair of spectacles for each one of us. Spectacles with the Irish tricolour flag painted on to the lenses. He jibed that if we wore them throughout the whole of the meeting then maybe we would begin to see the world in the same way that he and his colleagues did! What lenses are you looking through and what needs to change?

Hearing other voices

What voices are you listening to as a leader? Why not take a moment to make a list of ten people that you have listened to most often in the last month?

What do you notice about their race, their gender, their class, their age, their background, their privilege, their nationality, their language? How is that shaping who you are as an individual and as an organization?

In the international NGO that I led, we deliberately and regularly invited our overseas partners to lead devotions and prayers. To listen to the voices of our beneficiaries, and to have their stories front and central in our minds, changed who we were. To hear the Bible read with different emphasis and to hear people pray in a different language was just liberating.

It changed how we thought about the work that we did. It changed how thankful we were for the work we were engaged in. It enabled us to enter into pain and suffering like never before, and to cry and to weep – and to laugh and dance with those who had no voice but brought great joy and grace into our lives.

Listening to dissenting voices

True wisdom doesn't see opposition in dissenting voices, but opportunity.

Who is speaking into your life with words of challenge?

Who is speaking into your life from the perspective of a child?

Who is speaking into your life from a different theological perspective?

Who is speaking into your life from a different geography?

Who is speaking into your life from an older person's perspective?

Who is speaking into your life from a different economic outlook?

Who is speaking into your life from a different political perspective?

My first director-level boss in British Telecom said at our first meeting something along the lines of:

> I don't want to spend much time talking about what you have done, because everyone tells me you are great at your job. But I do want to spend most of the time at these meetings talking about someone you have met for the first time, from our industry, outside of BT.

I didn't appreciate at the time the power of those words or the way in which they would shape my route to becoming a CEO. You see, they taught me the power of perspective and of seeing things through the benefit of others' experience and insight.

Listening well

'The overarching principle of effective listening is to seek first to understand, then to be understood,' says Rick Fulwiler, a programme director at the Harvard T. H. Chan School of Public Health, and the former Director of Health and Safety Worldwide at Procter and Gamble. Fulwiler lists five key barriers to effective listening:

1 **prejudging the person you need to listen to** making assumptions based on their gender, language, background;
2 **formulating a response or rebuttal before someone is finished with their message** wanting to be heard more than to listen, wanting to sound knowledgeable;
3 **listening just for facts** missing the vital clues that come through emotions and body language;
4 **misunderstanding cultural cues** lacking the knowledge to be able to pick up on the nuanced cultural clues that reveal deeper levels of understanding;
5 **multitasking** being distracted by your phone and not giving the person in front of you the full benefit of your attention.

Here are some things that you can do to improve your listening skills and develop a listening posture.

- **Remain curious by asking good questions** Keep a bank of good questions you hear other people asking – the information you receive is highly influenced by the questions you ask.
- **Make notes of emotions as well as facts** I draw a right-hand margin on my notebook and note emotions there that I am picking up. You can draw or have icons if you like – or just write the words. These can be your emotions and those you are sensing from the person you are talking to.
- **Research culture** *The Culture Map* by Erin Meyer is a fantastic place to start as it unpacks how people think and lead across global cultures.[6]

- **Ask others if you are a good listener** If they say that you are not, ask them what they feel keeps you from being one and concentrate on those weak points.
- **Seek first to understand** Always remind yourself that you have more to learn in every situation and that just one extra fact can change the whole way that you view a situation or a person.

Speaking out on behalf of others

Building on what Justin covered in the last chapter on 'Speaking up', can I as a white Welsh male living in England, speak on behalf of women, or of black people in the UK? Can I as a white evangelical Christian talk on behalf of a marginalized Muslim community? Of course not. That would be presumptuous and paternalistic.

Even when I have listened to them, and listened really well, and sought to enter into their world, I can only start to understand the pain, the struggles, the humanity that is theirs and theirs alone.

However, this doesn't mean there is nothing that I can do.

First, I can create the spaces in which these voices are heard. I can choose to use my privilege and platform and give it away to others so that they can speak. I can quote them, involve them, give way to them and promote them.

Second, I can be an ally of their causes, aligning myself and being a powerful voice alongside them in speaking out for issues that are of concern to them.

One of the great joys of speaking to churches and conferences about the work that we did in international development was to give that platform away to beneficiaries and partners. To recognize that this work was not about me but about them. That people's lives were enriched as they heard the story of a young boy, who having received a shoebox gift as a child in an orphanage, was now able to come full circle and be one of those who was working night and day to bring joy and hope and life into the lives of millions of children around the world – including back in his own country of Rwanda.

The audiences I spoke to would never have received that from me. They would never have experienced the depths of pain and agony of a young boy who lost his parents in the midst of genocide – however well I told the story on his behalf.

We need to give away our platforms so that these stories are heard. So that the stories of the victims of abuse, genocide and war are listened to and so that systemic change can come.

Giving your organization ears

It's all very well listening as a leader, but what about your organization – how is it listening to other voices and remaining open to challenge and inspiration and development? How is it hearing the voices from outside?

Here are some great questions to start asking about your organization, whether you have just started working there or you are the CEO.

1 How diverse is your board of directors/trustees/leadership team? Does it adequately represent the constituency you are working with – its donors, beneficiaries, supporters, customers, clients?
2 How is selection of new board members/trustees/leadership team implemented? Is there adequate scope to bring on others who are not already known by the current directors?
3 How is your organization listening to its beneficiaries/supporters/ members? Is there adequate space to listen to a wide set of voices in the normal pattern of organizational life?
4 How is your organization listening to those that historically it may have ignored? Is there space to listen to those who have been hurt, those who are on the margins, or those who have been ignored?
5 How is your organization listening to minorities represented within it? What support and peer groups are there? How are the minorities represented in the decision-making of the organization?
6 How are you utilizing exit interviews for staff to pick up general trends of staff whose voices are not being heard?
7 What independent routes are available for those who need to have a confidential conversation? Where do people go if they have concerns? How are you and others around you making it easy for people to lift their voice?

Reflections

1 What are your default lenses for looking at issues and how can you look at those issues from a different perspective?
2 What other voices do you need to speak into your life?
3 How can you help your organization to hear other voices?

'Today when I look at Robben Island, I see it as a celebration of the struggle and a symbol of the finest qualities of the human spirit, rather than as a monument to the brutal tyranny and oppression of apartheid.'

NELSON MANDELA, MY ROBBEN ISLAND

6

Sitting with victims and survivors

JUSTIN HUMPHREYS

On the wall at the top of the stairs leading to my home office, I have a large, framed lithograph print of Nelson Mandela's written and hand-signed reflections of his time on Robben Island. It is a limited edition item and, although expensive to buy, it was separated from the rather more expensive pieces of artwork that he painted of the island, each of which convey a different message about the polaric nature of freedom and oppression. In these few words, Mandela provides me with a daily challenge every time I leave and enter my office – it is deliberately sobering to be reminded of one's struggles, the injustices that have been perpetrated and the way in which we try to forge ahead regardless in an attempt to see something good emerge and take shape.

When considering Mandela's particular experience, I am continually re-acquainted with the cold reality that his suffering was based in the notion that, for some inexplicable reason, white skin was superior to black skin. That the freedom of white people was secured at the expense of black people. This injustice is one of the greatest scourges on our race and remains very real today. It has no place within Christian life.

When I think about the experiences of people like Mandela, Biko and the countless everyday heroes of our time fighting their respective battles – whether that be racial discrimination, church-based abuse or gender inequality (and many other examples) – I am often faced with the question of what it is that represents the active ingredient in a person's experience or character that leads them to be a survivor. The thing that enables them to rise above, look beyond and carry on. As painful as it may be, it can be important to make the distinction between victims and survivors in any context as there is likely to be a fundamental difference in their perspective and approach to the challenges of life.

Seeking to understand something of their experience is what enables us to engage with them empathically. In my many years of working with those who have been harmed and abused in both intra-familial and extra-familial or institutional situations, it is this desire to be able to understand something of their pain that often makes the difference. We will never fully understand another person, particularly when they have been subjected to horrific trauma, abuse or long-standing oppression, but what is essential is that we take the time to sit with them for a while and maybe just listen.

Relationally connected

As leaders, this idea of 'sitting with' may be a difficult one. How many times have we fallen into the trap of thinking there is too much to do and not enough time in which to do it? Neglecting to sit with others, especially those who are struggling or experiencing some form of injustice, is a missed opportunity. Why do I say this? If we are to thrive in any circumstance, it is often based on our ability to experience the power of being relationally connected to others. The sense that we get from knowing we are valued and appreciated by another human being may literally make a life or death difference for some.

I am privileged to be able to speak with survivors of church-based abuse quite often. One of these survivors comes to mind particularly: he has told me repeatedly that his life has been so destroyed by his experience that he has contemplated taking his own life on many occasions. He often feels that he has nothing left and little motivation to continue fighting the Church for recognition. For him, the difference of knowing that people are there – that they will listen, that they care and are trying their best to understand his pain and with him do something about it – is literally a factor that keeps him alive.

In that place of taking time to sit with others, we not only have the chance to convey that sense of value, we also have the privilege of finding real gold in the life and experience of that person. In his six principles of coaching leadership (in his book *Mining for Gold*), Tom Camacho states that all true thriving is relational and that the trinitarian relationship of

Father, Son and Holy Spirit is the best example of this.[1] There is something deeply powerful about learning from another person's suffering. That's not that I'm necessarily advocating that we go in search of those who are suffering, but the richness of learning that comes from being vulnerable with another person, creating a safe place and allowing them to be vulnerable with us cannot be overstated.

We are often in such a hurry to get from one place to another (metaphorically or otherwise) that we fail to take the time to sit and invest in someone else or at least take the time to learn from others. When Jesus recognized this and felt the need to 'withdraw' from the crowds, we might be forgiven for thinking he was exhausted and just wanted to be alone with himself. In actual fact, he needed to be *with* the Father (Luke 5.15–16):

> Yet the news about him spread all the more, so that crowds of people came to hear him and to be healed of their illnesses. But Jesus often withdrew to lonely places and prayed.

Jesus 'often' withdrew. This is important. Yes, granted that he often went to quiet places to escape the chaos and busyness of life, but invariably it was to spend time in the presence of his Father (he prayed), rather than true solitude with his own thoughts – and it happened often. This relational connectedness was an essential part of his ministry and ability to keep going in the face of many trying circumstances. You see, we sustain both ourselves and others in these purposeful interactions – they are life-giving.

Finding the place of discomfort

As important as it was for Jesus to spend time with his Father, I guess he was mostly seeking the wisdom and direction of someone he knew deeply. That's not to say that Jesus would always have liked what his Father had to say (remember the conversation in the garden of Gethsemane in the days before his crucifixion), but generally I don't think he was expecting challenge or confrontation in his usual interactions. But sometimes, maybe our best understanding of the world and others within it comes from the situations that do make us deeply uncomfortable. This is so important for any leader to grasp. Leadership is not for the faint-hearted or for the person who expects to coast through life on the back of others' achievements. In his snapshot of leadership, Seth Godin expresses this well:

> It's uncomfortable to stand up in front of strangers. It's uncomfortable to propose an idea that might fail. It's uncomfortable to challenge the status quo. It's uncomfortable to resist the urge to settle. When you identify the discomfort, you've found the place where a leader is needed.[2]

In my experience, some of the most uncomfortable and challenging situations have come when I have felt at the end of myself or have been forced to hear the stinging criticisms of others, or where I have been faced with hearing the most heartbreaking and complex stories in testimony by survivors of abuse. Of these, the stories of appalling experiences of abuse within the Church are the hardest to hear and bring the greatest challenge. Why is that? It is because I love the Church. I love God's people and it hurts deeply to see the damage that is done to those who have entrusted their lives (physically and spiritually) to its leaders, whether local, national or international, only to be wounded as a consequence.

When trust is misplaced and then abused by leaders, it sets a destructive undercurrent in motion that sweeps through any tribe or congregation, often with little visible sign. Being confronted with the reality of something that should be positive and life-enriching in fact being dysfunctional and destructive takes some courage to face. Approaching such challenges with any level of inert tribalism will not result in a successful and sustainable change in culture or direction. The leader must in these circumstances be prepared to challenge the status quo and be subject to the possible personal and professional consequences of that challenge.

When relational connectedness and discomfort collide

When George Floyd was killed by a police officer in Minneapolis, Minnesota, what rightly followed was a global tidal wave of outrage. The

#BlackLivesMatter campaign regained momentum and was brought firmly into the consciousness of the world once again. As I reflect on the events of this period, I remain appalled at this example of injustice. I also recognize that it was a period of great discomfort for me as a white male leader in the UK.

Again, why was that? It is because I was brought face to face with the painful reality that I had failed to exercise my leadership in a way that championed the cause of black people (or people of colour), that saw them clearly and fought for them. I was guilty of countless acts of omission (rather than commission) where I had not been sufficiently alert to the racial inequality, oppression and disadvantage that had without doubt existed around me for my entire life. That despicable acts of racial hatred and violence could occur in the society in which I live, challenged me to the core and literally made me feel sick.

This brought me to a crucial point – when my relational connectedness collided with my discomfort. It occurred one day during the first COVID-19 lockdown in the UK. I was discussing the Black Lives Matter campaign in the wake of George Floyd's death with a black colleague. Sitting and listening to her recount the everyday challenges and fears of being a single mother of two young black boys literally broke me. In that moment, as I faced my colleague, totally choked, I just could not utter a single word for what felt like a painful eternity. I had again been brought face to face with the reality of someone else's world and it was in many ways so different from mine. Was this a time for me to exercise leadership? What was I to do? There was a raging injustice right in front of me.

My decision at that point was to ensure that I created the opportunity to sit and spend time with my black colleagues to understand their perspective on the world and particularly the part of it that I had some influence on. I had further discussions with other black colleagues and friends and, again, I was brought to look in the mirror and consider my part in what had been and what could be in the future.

Often, our instinctive reaction when facing anticipated challenges is to opt for the easy path (or at least the path of least pain or resistance). I would encourage you in those moments as a leader not to shy away from the difficult path. It may be painful, but there is valuable learning to be found. In fact, Chand would say that 'if you're not hurting, you're not leading'.[3] In this he suggests that there is a leadership journey that must be travelled – through growth that requires change, that change brings loss and that loss will inevitably bring pain. He therefore suggests that if we are to grow as individuals and leaders, we must expect pain.

As Cathy Madavan puts it, 'Going through it is not optional'.[4] Facing our fears and confronting the pain is part of something important – it may be our pain or the pain of someone else (that is external pain or internal pain). Without it we limit our own growth and success. I would also add to the earlier thoughts of Godin and say that if we are struggling to know where to start, we should seek out the places where relational connectedness and discomfort collide. That is where we are likely to find the pain and channel its effects to establish where effective and just leadership is required. It creates a productive collision (see Figure 3). But don't stop there. Use it as a foundation for what lessons can be learned and achieved elsewhere. This is only the beginning and an opportunity to plant good seed for sustainable future change and growth.

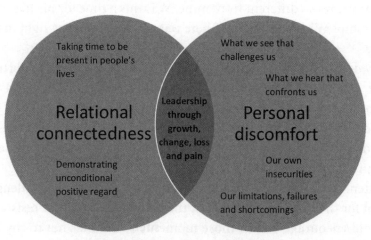

Figure 3 A productive collision

Learning lessons

Let's take some time to think about this idea of learning lessons for a moment. Often, one of our biggest mistakes can be to forget that the past can (and should) inform the present and the present should inform the future. Taking time to rest and then wrestle with an issue that we face, and to look back at where we may have come across anything that is either similar, or that has transferable learning, is a gift. We are all too often in too much of a hurry to get to the solution, so that we can be free to move on to the next challenge. I am as guilty of this as the next person. In fact, it reminds me of the results of one of those personality testing exercises that I undertook many years ago. You know the sort – the ones that after having answered what seems like a million questions, you are presented with an analysis that scares you half to death because it's so accurate?

On this occasion, I had gone through the exercise as part of a two-day assessment for an executive-level role that I had applied for within the organization I was already working in. It had not only been a long list of questions, but had included observed role play simulating a boardroom scenario. To cut a long story short, when I was presented with the document that told me all about my strengths and weaknesses based on the two days of exercises and analysis, one thing hit me hardest and has stayed with me ever since: it said that I had a short attention span and, although this enabled me to be extremely focused in the moment (which incidentally seemed to lend itself well to project-based work), I had a tendency to get bored and lose interest, as I would begin to start looking at the next thing. As I reflected for a while, this was, indeed, scarily accurate. My desire for results was strong. My ability to create and cast vision for what could be was proven. But both these things had to be held in tension with the fact that they also impeded my ability to stay in the moment long enough to find the nuggets of gold that could make all the difference to what I was working on.

Since this discovery, I have continually reminded myself of the fact that much of the work we do in pursuit of justice takes time – often lots of time. There are rarely 'quick wins' in my experience in working for and alongside those who have suffered institutional harm. The problems, behaviours and cultures that lead to such harm are usually deeply embedded and extremely resistant to change.

An elevated position

It is so important that we slow down and take time to reflect and make the best use of what the past and present might be telling us. The urge to race ahead, only to find we have reached an impasse without all the knowledge and information that would be helpful to us, leads to frustration, disappointment and a need to retrace our footsteps (as I described in Chapter 7 of my last book *Escaping the Maze of Spiritual Abuse*[5]). Taking time to navigate difficult situations and reach an elevated position from which we can see more clearly, guide more sensitively and speak more compassionately as we assist others, is a crucial part of the process towards finding justice for those who have been wronged and identifying lessons to be learned for all concerned.

This is why one of the most important areas of work that I have been leading through thirtyone:eight in recent times has been conducting 'Independent Lessons Learned Reviews' for organizations where harm and abuse has been caused by leaders and influencers. Such work is distinct from an investigation in strict terms as it takes a more systems-focused approach to identifying what has happened, how it happened and what lessons need to be learned as a result to prevent a repeat (in that environment or elsewhere, given that the lessons can often be applied more broadly than within the commissioning organization). These are incredibly detailed assignments that have to be navigated with extreme care and attention – particularly in terms of spending sufficient time with victims and survivors who have taken the courageous step to share their stories with our expert review teams. The outcome of such work has to be that an effectively elevated position is found, from which a better view and understanding can be gained. This takes time and lots of it. Sitting with people to hear their accounts and reflections is a huge privilege.

Eusebeigenic sin

Invariably, when working with victims and survivors of abuse within a church or faith-based context, their motivation is not financial compensation (although for some this is important and necessary).

Rather, it is that what they have experienced is acknowledged and therefore validated and that lessons can be learned so that others should not have to suffer in the same way. The opportunity to learn such lessons should be embraced and embodied wholeheartedly because the damage that can be done in religious contexts has the most deep and profound impact on the victim.

In fact, the very existence of some forms of wrongdoing (or sin) can only exist in this religious context and the spiritual impact on one's soul demands special attention. In his excellent exploration of what justice really means in Christian life, Ken Wytsma reflects powerfully on the concept of the sins of the righteous.[6] In this, he refers to the concept created by Eugene Peterson of 'eusebeigenic sin'. Drawn from the two Greek words *eusebeia* (meaning 'godly' or 'devout') and *latrogenic* (meaning 'created by the healer') – he makes this very point:

Eusebeigenic sin is difficult to detect because the sin is always embedded in words and acts that have the appearance of being righteous, godly, devout . . . [It] is mostly picked up in a place associated with righteousness, a church or bible study or prayer meeting.'[7]

In other words, the harm that is caused by the sins of those who profess to carry the spirit of God is unique. Wytsma points out that we read in Scripture that Jesus criticized the Pharisees for this very thing: self-righteousness, legalism and piety causing distress to others (Matthew 23.23–39). It is also the case that taking the Apostle Paul's view of the body (being at one with the mind and spirit) means we must accept the depth of harm caused when one member of the Christian body abuses another. This is so eloquently articulated by Paula Gooder:

We must take with the utmost seriousness the consequences of the way in which we relate to others . . . Christian communities around the world live with the unremitting shame of the fact that members of the body of Christ have abused others . . . If we accept Paul's premise that our identity is formed by relationship, and if that relationship has been abused, then the body of Christ becomes as ugly and toxic as it can be.[8]

Why would anybody who has experienced harm to the degree that many have not want to do all they can to assist others to avoid it? If victims remain engaged in any form with a community of faith that has been so destructive to them, we should see that as being a huge advantage in finding our way back to individual and collective repentance, reparation and wholeness. Overlooking or even dismissing this motivation, and using the cloak of financial and reputational cost as a means for derailing a righteous pursuit of justice, is a further abuse of victims. We must do all we can to aid and empower those with such a righteous desire for justice!

Victim or survivor?

So returning to this fundamental question, it is important to be clear that no blanket rule should be applied. Those who have experienced trauma, harm and abuse will find the best way to express their experiences and identify themselves. This should never be about attaching labels to people, but seeing the person who might be sitting in front of us and achieving some connection with them where they are.

In fact, an important place to start would be to allow any person in the aftermath of a traumatic event to find the words and arrive at a position where they ascribe to themselves whichever identifier feels appropriate. This may of course change over time and should not necessarily be seen as a binary 'choice'. Supporting people in this process and beyond will sometimes come laced with challenge and complexity, and may be difficult, but we must be prepared to go there as leaders and helpers.

I have considered this question of victim and survivor quite a lot over the years (as you might imagine in the area of work I am in). It is not an easy one to get to the bottom of and I almost feel some sense of nervousness about attempting to find a clear distinction. I hope that what I am about to say will be received with an understanding that this may not ring true for everyone. In fact, there may well be other opposing views, but this has helped my own developing understanding on the subject.

When I consider the two words, the first thing that strikes me is that 'victim' says something about the here and now. An individual has been subjected to a harmful event about which they had no control. They have been victim to a situation or act. There is something about the word that suggests that person is held in that place, continuing to experience a lack of agency to rise above it. This is no criticism, but indicates they are still subject to that experience, such that moving beyond it is problematic, if not seemingly impossible. When I read the word 'survivor', I am faced with a much different picture. It doesn't in any way diminish the destructive power of a harmful or traumatic event that has taken place, but it does indicate some ability to have made positive steps forward despite that event. In his latest work, Patrick Regan talks about his own view of how resilience is developed and used to assist a 'bouncing forward' and wonderfully describes it as follows:

> Bouncing forward means we don't stay in a constant state of crises, but we go on day by day, changed, and hopefully more accepting. We can't wipe the pain from our lives so we have a choice: try and ignore it and allow it to break us, or work with it and see if it can lead us somewhere new.[9]

Although not a sole or exclusive factor, having reflected on my own adverse childhood experiences, I see that there is real truth in this notion of forward movement and the level of determination required to achieve it. Patrick's words acknowledge the depth of pain, but are infused with words of tentative hope – and that's a wonderful thing!

It is important also to acknowledge that whatever our own personal life experience has been, we are never in a position where we can fully put ourselves in the shoes of another person (Simon explores this further in the next chapter). Our experience may have been similar, as far as we can discern, but it would be a mistake (even for those of us who are victims or survivors of past abuse) to assume that we therefore fully understand the pain and impact of abuse on the other person.

We must also be careful to resist the assumption that a self-identifying survivor may not have moments where their past experiences return to them with force, often triggered by current experiences, smells, sounds or other reminders that have the power to take them back. We must always do our very best to be patient, loving, gracious and persistent in our support of them.

This is an important principle in how we see and value each person. In fact, one of the greatest gifts we can receive when working in this extremely complex area of pursuing justice is that we are afforded the opportunity to hear the story of any victim or survivor, feel their pain and, in so doing, gain a glimpse of that person's world. We must then take that gift and use it sensitively with honesty and humility towards a shared objective; whether that is providing knowledgeable support, bringing necessary challenge and intervention, or driving towards greater systemic change.

Reflections

1 Who do you need to take time to sit with and hear their story of being a victim or survivor?
2 Where have you heard the stories of victims and survivors and now have an obligation to use that sensitively to drive towards greater systemic change?
3 Where do you need to face up to discomfort so that you can hear the stories you need to hear and create the relational connections you need to lead authentically?

Don't walk behind me; I may not lead.

Don't walk in front of me; I may not follow.

Just walk beside me and be my friend.

ALBERT CAMUS (ATTRIB.)

7

Walking the victim's/survivor's journey

SIMON BARRINGTON

You can't walk a mile in another's shoes

The common parlance when we are talking about having empathy for someone else's position is to imagine walking a mile in that person's shoes. Eat what he eats, live in her neighbourhood, experience famine and drought, go without healthcare for a month.

However, when it comes to walking the victim's/survivor's journey, it's an unhelpful ask to walk a mile in a survivor's shoes. You probably never could experience what that person experienced, and it would be patronizing to suggest that you have ever experienced anything like it. However, leaders with justice at their heart will desire to put themselves, as much as possible, into the experiences and stories of survivors. This starts with believing their stories. It's what thirtyone:eight asks supporters of their Safer Places Pledge to do.

Put survivors first

Too often we see cases where victims and survivors have not been believed, have been silenced or have been further abused by the response they have received. We will listen to victims and survivors and ensure we put their needs at the heart of any response.[1]

Just acknowledging a victim's story as a leader and taking it seriously is the first step in walking the journey, in coming alongside. We may not know what to say or how the journey will map out, but our very presence is a powerful statement. Being able to say, 'I may not know what you have experienced, but whatever happens, I will be here for you' is the greatest gift you can give someone.

Your very presence

I have known many times in my international development work when the power of our presence has been felt. Where just 'turning up' gave a positive statement that the people we were visiting were not forgotten, not abandoned, not despised by the international community.

As an agency, we were determined to go where no one else was working – to go off the beaten track and to come alongside victims and survivors of war, famine, disease and poverty.

Whether that was in Foya District in Northern Liberia, where we were the only charity working in community development, or on the border between Sudan and South Sudan in the refugee camps of Yida and Blue Nile or in the camps in Northern Iraq, where Yazidis who had fled Syria and Iraq shelter from war and persecution. Whenever you turn up in the unexpected places, the message is the same: thank you for coming. Thank you for taking the time and effort to come and walk alongside us, to understand our plight, to take time to notice what is happening to us and to listen. As a leader, your very presence with victims or survivors speaks volumes – to them and to those you are leading.

Baroness Caroline Cox knows this only too well. Over a lifetime of speaking out on behalf of those who have no voice, she has championed just turning up in the most unexpected places. Climbing mountains to reach forgotten people, traversing rivers, climbing out of helicopters and putting her own life at risk – even into her eighties – to raise the profile of victims of persecution and human rights abuse.

In a conflict zone, Baroness Cox once met a leader who said, 'Thank you. You have come to us [and, just like Doubting Thomas], you have put your hands into the wounds of our suffering. Now you believe; go and tell.'[2]

The purpose of her travels is always to learn so that she can help to educate others, including those in Parliament in the UK, about the plight of the voiceless.

So who are you being present for?
Who needs your presence right now?
Whose story needs to be believed?
Who needs to be listened to?

Walking alongside

Here are some tips that I've picked up from walking alongside victims, listening to those who do so professionally[3] and by making lots of mistakes!

1 Be aware of your own safeguarding guidance and principles.
2 Be culturally aware and sensitive to the individual.
3 Don't be shocked – prepare yourself to listen to and hear the words that are being spoken.
4 Don't judge. Ever.
5 Make every effort to be on the survivor's level – to be truly alongside.
6 When the survivor is talking or sharing – just listen.
7 Try to use 'we' and not 'you' or 'they'.
8 It's OK not to have answers.
9 See the survivor as a valuable person, worthy of love, care and respect – not someone defined by an event or series of events.
10 Try to look to the future.

The forgotten ones

It may well be that the survivor whose story needs to be believed is a survivor of non-recent events or certainly not something that is in vogue currently. Sometimes, the most poignant encounters I have had have been with survivors whose story has been an ongoing one, survivors whose story is not in the current news cycle.

Our television cameras and radio news programmes move on so quickly. From survivors of abuse, to refugees crossing the Channel, to Black Lives Matter, the Rohingya people in Myanmar or the Uighur Muslims in China – there are so many injustices and many others' stories are forgotten and not deemed worthy of making it to our television screens.

Take, for example, Internally Displaced People[4] in Azerbaijan. Most of these people fled from conflict with Armenia in Nagorno-Karabakh between 1988 and 1994. Nearly 30 years later, the Nagorno-Karabakh area is still in a state of legal limbo, with the Republic of Artsakh remaining de facto independent, but internationally unrecognized, while Armenian forces currently control approximately 9 per cent of Azerbaijan's territory outside the enclave. More than a million people have been displaced or become refugees as a result of the conflict.[5]

Imagine being displaced from your home for 30 years, not able to return. However you seek to rebuild your life, and however future generations are able to move on, the pain, anguish, loss and grief still remains real. I remember visiting many of the refugees who lived in disused railway carriages in Imishli – in 2008, fourteen years on from the conflict. At that point, they already felt forgotten by the international community and were finding it difficult to get any time and attention from governments to enable their case to be heard.

In our walking alongside victims and survivors, we must be careful not to simply follow the latest trend and the last news cycle. There is a faithfulness and godliness in walking alongside the forgotten ones who don't have column inches, who don't have Instagram accounts, who don't have large lobbying teams and advocacy programmes.

Psalm 146 reminds us not only that God is walking alongside the oppressed and the forgotten but also that he is 'faithful for ever'.

Blessed are those whose help is the God of Jacob,
    whose hope is in the LORD their God.
He is the Maker of heaven and earth,
    the sea, and everything in them –
    he remains faithful for ever.
He upholds the cause of the oppressed
    and gives food to the hungry.
The LORD sets prisoners free,
    the LORD gives sight to the blind,
the LORD lifts up those who are bowed down,
    the LORD loves the righteous.
The LORD watches over the foreigner

and sustains the fatherless and the widow,
>   but he frustrates the ways of the wicked.
The LORD reigns for ever,
>   your God, O Zion, for all generations.
Praise the LORD.
(Psalm 146.5–10)

Putting it into practice

So how, then, can we practise walking with victims and survivors? What are the practical ways in which we can walk with them? What should our posture be?

First, we must walk faithfully.

Second, we must walk humbly.

Third, we must walk with loving kindness.

Finally, we must walk hopefully.

Walking faithfully

She was 43 years old when I met her. It was 9 o'clock in the morning and the sun was already high in the sky and it looked like we were on for another scorching 40-degree day in rural Mozambique. I had risen a few hours earlier, showered and had breakfast. For her, the day had begun much earlier. At 4 a.m. Just like every other day. The 4 a.m. walk was her ritual. The walk for water – life-giving, scarce water. It was a 9-mile round trip with her sister, carrying 20-kg containers – as heavy as your airport luggage – on their heads. She then got her two boys ready for school and headed off to the fields to work, gathering maize for four hours until the heat of the day was unbearable. She would receive £2 in total for her back-breaking endeavours. Then she began to make dinner – some maize, rarely chicken, some beans, maybe some rice. Dinner for her, her boys and for the five orphans she cared for daily in her community. As if her life wasn't hard enough, it was the lives of the children who had no parents, the children whose families were the victims of HIV and AIDS, the children who were now heading up households, who broke her heart. And so she walked faithfully alongside them. Every day. In the midst of her own pain and anguish and the difficulties and trials of her own daily life, in one of the most inhospitable parts of creation. Daily walking. Daily coming alongside the orphans with dinner, help with homework, parental guidance and advice. When her head hit the mat at night, exhausted, she knew it would start again at 4 a.m. the following morning. Her name was Maria.

Maria the faithful, we might call her. Maria who walked faithfully alongside the HIV and AIDs orphans. Daily engaging, daily serving, daily coming alongside. Always there. Always present. Always providing.

There is so much here that mirrors the faithfulness of God. Faithful in trial, faithful in season and out of season. Faithful each day from the rising of the sun to the setting of the same. Persistent. Present. Walking alongside. Engaged. Patient. Persevering.

Faithful 'means that God will always do what he has said and fulfil what he has promised' (Grudem).[6]

Because God is faithful, we are to be faithful too in our outworking of justice. If we are to be justice-centred leaders, then we must be faithful in walking alongside victims and survivors. Doing what we say we will do and fulfilling our promises to those we have committed to walking alongside.

Some of the sweetest moments in our lives have been when those who have chosen to walk alongside us through the ups and downs of life – when tragedy hits, when calamity comes, when all seems lost – have come and just sat with us, quietly, and whispered, 'We are here for you. Whatever.'

Walking humbly

There is a humility required of justice-centred leaders that is clear in the Scriptures.

He has shown you, O mortal, what is good.
    And what does the LORD require of you?
To act justly and to love mercy
    and to walk humbly with your God.
(Micah 6.8)

Micah is clear that this is a requirement of God for us. Not a gentle ask, or even just a suggestion. Rather, it is something that we are told to do.

Over the past few years, business leaders have been slowly waking up to the fact that it is servant-based leaders who walk in humility who bring out the best in other people. As Dan Cable puts it in his excellent article in the *Harvard Business Review*:

> To put it bluntly, servant-leaders have the humility, courage, and insight to admit that they can benefit from the expertise of others who have less power than them. They actively seek the ideas and unique contributions of the employees that they serve. This is how servant leaders create a culture of learning, and an atmosphere that encourages followers to become the very best they can.
>
> Humility and servant leadership do not imply that leaders have low self-esteem, or take on an attitude of servility. Instead, servant leadership emphasizes that the responsibility of a leader is to increase the ownership, autonomy, and responsibility of followers — to encourage them to think for themselves and try out their own ideas.[7]

If this is true in general leadership, then how much more so for the leader who is seeking to act justly and love mercy.

Edgar and Peter Schein in their book *Humble Leadership: The power of relationships, openness and trust* set out four levels of relationship.

Level Minus 1: total impersonal domination and coercion.
Level 1: transactional role and rule-based supervision, service and most forms of 'professional' relationships.
Level 2: personal cooperative, trusting relationships, as in friendships and in effective teams.
Level 3: emotionally intimate, total mutual commitments.[8]

They explain that humble leadership can only happen at Level 2:

> The essence of Level 2 is that the other person, whether boss, employee, peer or partner, moves from being seen as a 'role' – a

partial or undifferentiated person who must be kept 'professionally distant' – to being seen as a *whole* person with whom we can develop a more personal relationship around shared goals and experiences.[9]

In the context of walking with victims and survivors, this concept of Level 2 humble leadership is vitally important, because it allows us to move beyond the labels of victims, survivors, helpers and advocates to seeing each person as fully made in the image of God, with huge potential to thrive. We can also begin to see our relationship with them as less of the 'professional' helper and much more of the faithful friend, who is also fully seen.

Walking with loving kindness

In Micah 6.8, as we saw, there is a call to love mercy. In the original Hebrew, the word translated is '*hesed*', which means 'loving kindness'. *Hesed* is often used to describe God's relationship with us. *Hesed* is a much richer word than 'mercy'. There is also so much more here than just love and kindness. It is loving kindness, wrapped up in a covenant commitment.

God's *hesed* denotes his persistent and unconditional tenderness, kindness and mercy – a relationship in which he seeks after all people with love and mercy. As Dale Ralph Davis puts it in his commentary on 1 Samuel.20, 'it is not merely love, but loyal love; not merely kindness, but dependable kindness; not merely affection, but affection that has committed itself.'[10]

The call to justice-centred leadership is indeed a call to *hesed*. A call to unconditional tenderness, dependable kindness, loyal love and affection that has committed itself to the well-being of the other person. It is this sense of commitment, of covenant, that sets it apart. And it is an action-orientated word, as Will Kynes of the C. S. Lewis Institute points out:

> Further, *hesed* is never merely an abstract feeling of goodwill but always entails practical action on behalf of another, whether that involves the restored cupbearer putting in a good word to the Pharaoh for Joseph (Gen. 40.14), Bethuel giving his daughter Rebekah in marriage (Gen. 24.49–51), or the Israelite army sparing the family of Rahab (Josh. 2.12–13).[11]

Walking hopefully

Walking hopefully with a victim or survivor means:

- seeing the best;
- believing the best;
- hoping for the best;
- working towards a better future.

Often victims or survivors have been put in a position where hope is a rare commodity. They will often describe their situations as 'without hope or a future' or 'hopeless'.

Hoping for the best doesn't mean believing in fairy tales or pretending that there is not real hurt, real injustice, real pain and anger. Far from it. Hoping and working for a better future means working for justice, working for mercy, sometimes working towards forgiveness, sometimes reconciliation.

Hoping for the best also doesn't mean trying to see a light at the end of the tunnel. Rather, it means starting to help people see some light in the tunnel. That even in the darkest of moments there can be laughter as well as tears, there can be connection, there can be days which seem brighter than the darkest of days, even if the brightness is dimmed.

Our role as justice-centred leaders is not to be the hope, but to point to the hope. Not to be the bringer of hopeful solutions or escape routes or resolutions – although sometimes we may be able to do that – but, rather, to help bring perspective, help bring comfort, help bring faith that the future has possibilities.

Meanwhile, we chose to walk forwards, alongside, whatever the future holds, walking fully in the present, faithfully and with humility.

Reflections

1 Who needs the gift of your presence right now?
2 Where in your relationships do you need to move from Level 1 to Level 2 leadership?
3 What does exercising loving kindness mean for you in your context?

JUST LEADERSHIP: POSTURE

If there is no friendship with them
and no sharing of the life of the
poor, then there is no authentic
commitment to liberation, because
love only exists among equals.

GUSTAVO GUTIERREZ[1]

8

Practising proximity

SIMON BARRINGTON

At the heart of the Christian gospel is the truth that God comes close to us. As J. B. Phillips puts it:

> God may thunder His commands from Mount Sinai and men may fear yet remain at heart exactly as they were before. But let a man once see his God down in the arena as a Man, – suffering, tempted, sweating, and agonized, finally dying a criminal's death – and he is a hard man indeed who is untouched.[2]

Or, to quote that great preacher, Bono, of U2:

> Just as God was working out redemptive history at the cross, God is [also] in the slums, God is also in the cardboard boxes where the poor play house . . . God is in the silence of a mother who has infected her child with a virus that will end both their lives . . . God is in the cries heard under the rubble of war . . . God is in the debris of wasted opportunity and lives, God is with the children, and God is with us if we are with them.[3]

God has come close – in the person of Jesus Christ. This is not just a matter of justice being at the heart of the character of God, but of God coming up close and personal to injustice in human form and having experienced the emotions, the heartbreak, the pain and the agony of seeing injustice and experiencing injustice.

This is our pattern and our model, one that is a constant challenge to us as leaders to 'enter in' to the zone of discomfort and to come out from behind our anonymous screens and our ordered and structured lives to experience the 'messiology' (as George Verwer describes it) of rolling our sleeves up and getting stuck in.

I will always remember the first shoebox gift I delivered to a child in an orphanage in Azerbaijan, back in 2003. The pictures are drawn into my memory with indelible ink. Initially we walked into the roofless kitchen of that orphanage and observed children aged between three and eleven being served lunch into their bare hands because there were no plates or knives or forks available. Even that didn't prepare me though for the living conditions I found in the children's bedrooms. We met one young girl – let's call her Anya – who was nine years old. She had lived in the orphanage all her life. There were no toys, no books, no warm hugs for Anya – and it showed in her eyes. There is a dull, blank, cold and grey look in the eyes of children who have not experienced the warmth and compassion of adults that is haunting and disturbing. Anya took us to her bedroom, which had four beds in it for twelve children.

It was −20 °C outside and snow lay on the ground as we sat on Anya's bed, which she shared with three other girls, and opened her simple shoebox with simple gifts. There were burns on her legs from getting too close to the wood-burning fire in the middle of the room to keep warm.

I arrived home from that trip on Christmas Eve to put a Christmas stocking in front of my fireplace in my nice centrally heated home and proceeded upstairs to read a goodnight story to my seven-year-old daughter as I tucked her into her single bed under her nice warm duvet. 'There, but for the grace of God . . .' had never had such a powerful meaning.

Of course, Anya had received charity – and it put a smile on her face – not justice. I'm only too well aware of that. But I had come face to face with injustice and looked it in the eye and I was forever changed.

If we are to be leaders with justice in our hearts, we must look it in the eye, we must hear the stories, we must, as a matter of routine, have the courage to get into the mess.

You don't have to go to Azerbaijan to do that though. I remember the CEO of one of the largest Christian charities I know reminding us at a conference that his organization may be providing food and shelter for millions around the world, but he could be just as guilty of walking past injustice on his street corner as the next man or woman. There is injustice in my town right now – sexual abuse, human trafficking, County Lines, child poverty to name a few examples. I don't need to go very far to encounter it, but it does take a consistent, intentional effort. It's a conscious decision to enter into relationship – not just to flirt with injustice but to encounter it and to come into relationship with those who are enduring it on a day-to-day basis.

So, how can we do that?

Injustice caused by a series of broken relationships

In his brilliant book, *Walking with the Poor,* Bryant L. Myers, Professor of Transformational Development at Fuller Theological Seminary and formerly Vice President of Global Strategy at World Vision, developed a framework that is extremely helpful in thinking through injustice as a series of broken relationships that need to be redeemed by bringing them into closer proximity.[4] According to Myers, poverty and injustice are caused by a series of broken relationships:

relationship with God = poverty of spiritual intimacy
relationship with self = poverty of being
relationship with others = poverty of community
relationship with creation = poverty of stewardship

These broken relationships affect the economic, political, social and religious systems that people live with – they affect all of life. All of us suffer from these broken relationships. Our brokenness affects the way we approach justice and other people.

So how are these relationships mended and justice restored? A first step can be to increase our proximity. Our relationship with God is restored because he chose to come close to us. This then has an impact on every other relationship. As a consequence:

• our relationship with self is restored, as we chose to understand ourselves as being made in the image of God;

- our relationship with others is restored, as we come close to them and build authentic, real community;
- our relationship with creation is restored, as we chose to come close and understand our stewarding responsibility.

So how can we restore proximity with others? How can we come close so that the abuse and exploitation of others becomes impossible because we are in close proximity and relationship with them?

The Relational Proximity Framework

The Relationships Foundation (at: <www.relationshipsfoundation.org>) is a think tank for a better-connected society, based in Cambridge in the UK. It was set up twenty-five years ago to develop relational thinking and engage with policymakers. The foundation studies the effects that culture, business and government have on relationships and creates new ideas for strengthening social connections and campaign on issues where relationships are being undermined.

Its key model for understanding relational health and for enabling individuals and organizations to focus in on intentionally improving the quality and health of those relationships is the 'Relational Proximity Framework'. The framework has been used in prisons, healthcare systems, schools and businesses to help people to form longer-lasting, equity-based and stronger relationships. It has also been used in peace-making on the Korean peninsula and in South Sudan to bring what would appear to be two unreconcilable parties together to dialogue about a common future and overcome the injustices of the past.

The five dimensions of the Relational Proximity Framework are encounter, storyline, multiplexity, parity and purpose. Let's take each one of them in turn and explore how reducing the distance between two people in a relationship can help us to engage well with the thinking, emotions and behaviour of the other.

Encounter

First, there is communication and how it builds that sense of connectedness. Do the ways in which you communicate (such as face to

96

face, email, text) help to avoid misunderstanding and create a sense of connection?

Our default is to encounter injustice remotely. It takes courage to encounter it face to face. To enter a warzone; to be a safeguarding officer; to be at the forefront of identifying human slavery in the UK or trafficking or domestic violence. This is for the selfless and the well-meaning, for the passionate and the purposeful. Most of us, if we are honest, would rather sit in front of our TV, newspaper, computer, tablet or mobile phone and see from a distance.

Having a posture of leaning in and an intentionality of encounter is a must. A group of men from several local churches decided to find out for themselves what the real issues were with being homeless in our town. They took to the streets themselves for four nights. They went and talked to the homeless, but also experienced what it was like to be moved on from doorway to shelter. They also found out what services were and weren't on offer – from food to shelter – and what barriers there were to access them.

They found it an enlightening experience and one that has shaped the way that they are now seeking to respond and come alongside. Driven by passion and service, they now see the real gaps in provision, the real issues faced. What's more, they have made real friendships with homeless people across the town. Friendships that have been birthed in weekly drop-ins and weekly encounters have now become real, intimate friendships. It's a hard road, but an encounter that has changed them, dispelled myths and created a new sense of connection and relationship.

Storyline

Second, to think about the time and story of a relationship. Do the various interactions over time build a sense of momentum, growth, stability and, ultimately, a sense of belonging and loyalty?

In issues of justice, storyline is so important. My personal prejudices because of the history of my interactions on this subject may well be a historic impediment to me coming into proximity with the issue of injustice. My theological or cultural position on an issue, the stereotyping of the 'other' and cultural inertia mean that greater lengths of time may be required to come into close proximity with a community.

RM Surveys
Get to know them

For example, the historic position of evangelicals on women in leadership meant that it took time for me to move my position to one of not only accepting but also celebrating the gifting of women in leading the Church and particularly in preaching. My storyline with this issue has taken time to move from negativity and opposition to warm embrace, and many of my unconscious biases have had to be challenged and worked through in the process.

Storyline also recognizes that the relational proximity is a two-way street. I may feel that I want to come into proximity with an issue, but the historical baggage I carry may prevent that proximity from happening, even though my intentions and motives are positive and well-meaning. My very gender, race, language and membership of a cultural grouping may mean that the journey through time of a relational proximity takes care, sensitivity, patience and discernment, and also that others may be better placed to move the injustice issue forwards first.

Multiplexity

Third, we consider the types of contexts that shape how we are known and our ability both to read a person and to manage a relationship. Do both of you know enough about each other to manage the relationship effectively?

As I write this, my life – like that of so many others – is consumed by Zoom calls. We are a year into a lockdown, in the middle of the coronavirus global pandemic in the UK. One thing that these Zoom calls have done is allowed me to see into my colleagues' homes in an unprecedented way! I've been fascinated by what's on their bookcases and walls and its been lovely to see their children and partners wandering in and out in the background, which has opened up different conversations about what is going on in their household.

We've seen one another from a different angle and our relationships are richer for it. So often our perspective on justice issues is seen through a single lens – maybe the lens of a particular newspaper or charity that has a certain political leaning or nuanced viewpoint that they are trying to get across. Every so often a reporter such as Louis Theroux or Stacey Dooley comes along and opens up a whole new perspective on the issues faced by an individual or a community. A campaigner such as Greta

Thunberg comes along and helps us to see climate change through the lens of a schoolchild and our knowledge and world-view are changed as a result.

A justice-filled leader needs to harness the different viewpoints available and develop a deep curiosity if proximity is to be maintained and deepened over time. Ask great questions, get great answers is the mantra. One interesting experiment which assists that at the moment is the concept of the Human Library (at: <www.humanlibrary.org>). Its motto is 'unjudge someone'. It works by creating a safe framework for personal conversations that can help to challenge prejudice, aim to help rid discrimination, prevent conflicts and contribute to greater human cohesion across social, religious and ethnic divisions.

This is done by creating a special dialogue room, where taboo topics can be discussed openly and without condemnation. A place where people who would otherwise never talk find room for conversation. The concept here is that everyone is a human book who can be 'borrowed' from the library and join in to a real conversation and be known through curiosity.

Parity

Fourth, to think about power and how it's used and experienced. Is authority used in ways that encourages participation, promotes fairness and conveys respect?

I first had to think hard about this when working in Swaziland. The only way to fly into that country from the UK is to fly into Johannesburg airport in South Africa and then take the 'Kings Jet' into the capital, Manzini. It's only a one-hour flight, but the very fact that you take it puts you in the elite – up there with the King. The vast majority of people in Swaziland have never flown. They have the highest rates of poverty and HIV and AIDS in the continent and the highest level of child-headed households.

As soon as you fly in and stay at a hotel, you are powerful. You don't even have to open your mouth or offer to pay for anything. You have power. This is the dilemma that so many 'aid' agencies have around the world. As soon as you are the one offering to help, offering to pay, offering to assist, then you are bringing knowledge, money, influence, insight that unbalances the relationship.

So if justice is about restoring relationships, however well-meaning you are and however charitable you are, you have to be extremely careful that you are not discouraging participation, promoting further unfairness and showing disrespect.

That's why, in many countries around the world, development organizations are developing and promoting community-based participation models that give ownership to local people, raise up community solutions to problems and focus on the relationship of 'walking together on a journey' rather than 'giving to resolve a problem'.

This takes more time, is deeply challenging to those of us who want to solve problems and want to feel good about helping, but ultimately these are more just, more proximate, more relational solutions.

We need to have a new conversation about power. As Andy Crouch so eloquently puts it:

What would a new conversation about power include? It would acknowledge, indeed insist, that power is a gift – the gift of a Giver who is the supreme model of power used to bless and serve. Power is not given to benefit those who hold it. It is given for the flourishing of individuals, peoples and the cosmos itself. Power's right use is especially important for the flourishing of the vulnerable, the members of the human family who most need others to use power well to survive and thrive: the young, the aged, the sick, and the dispossessed. Power is not the opposite of servanthood. Rather, servanthood, ensuring the flourishing of others, is the very purpose of power.[5]

Purpose

Last, to think about purpose, values and goals, and the degree to which they are shared in ways that bring synergy and motivation to a relationship. When examining the purposes of an organization and its people, how deep rooted are their intentions, or are the two parties pulling in different directions?

Churches in the UK have, over the last decade, done a huge amount to respond to social crisis in their communities. You only have to look at food banks, debt counselling centres, work with excluded children and mental health services to see the amazing outflow of compassion and care into society. In fact, it has been shown by the Cinnamon Network that this – from all faith groups – was worth £3 billion a year to the UK economy in 2019. That's two million people giving 384 million hours of voluntary time to social causes. Staggering.

However, the question we pose here is whether this has been done 'to' communities or 'with' communities. What a difference it would make if there was a commitment to work for the common good with our communities. This starts when we stop asking the question: 'What does our community need that the Church can provide?' and start asking the question, 'What can we do together to ensure the flourishing of our community?'

This is riskier, it involves coming closer to people and to asking ourselves some hard questions. To be willing to be changed by our encounter, to maybe have to re-examine our beliefs and values, to dig under the skin of our outward veneer of having it all together and to start to be moulded by our joint humanity and our desire to pray for the good of the city/town/village/community.

Developing a 'shared purpose' was shown in my research to be the highest desire of millennial leaders.[6] To be invited into a conversation where the end is unknown, where the goal is relationship and journey, and where the outcome is the increased well-being of all involved.

Now you've seen it, you just can't walk away

As a fundraiser for a large charity, one of the biggest challenges I had was not to allow someone to walk out of a fundraising dinner or event without giving. You see, we forget quickly, even when exposed to the most horrific injustices. I could bring donors to the point of tears in the middle of a presentation on atrocities in South Sudan or Mozambique or Northern Iraq, yet by the time they were in their taxis or having breakfast the following morning, a million new things had crowded into their lives and the moment of proximity was gone. When we are brought close, we have an obligation to act and to act promptly on what we have seen.

Reflections

1 How close to injustice have you come and how could you increase that proximity through encounter, storyline, multiplexity, parity and purpose?
2 What are your unconscious biases and how can you identify where they may be blocking you from tackling justice issues?
3 What have you seen but forgotten about and need to act on now?

Generosity is the flower of justice.

NATHANIEL HAWTHORNE[1]

9

Giving generousl

SIMON BARRINGTON

Why, in a book on justice, are we talking about generosity? We have in our minds that justice is about 'legal fairness', and we tend to think of generosity more in terms of charity, sharing and giving and linked to the biblical concept of mercy rather than justice. In fact, you could be forgiven for thinking that mercy was the polarity of justice rather than its close companion.

Yet, as Tim Keller points out in his book *Generous Justice*, the two are close neighbours and intertwined. Actually, he goes further and argues that generosity is one of the hallmarks of living justly. In Scripture they are frequently interlinked. For instance, this famous passage in Isaiah moves seamlessly from loosing the chains of justice to feeding the hungry:

> Is not this the kind of fasting I have chosen:
> to loose the chains of injustice
>   and untie the cords of the yoke,
> to set the oppressed free
>   and break every yoke?
> Is it not to share your food with the hungry
>   and to provide the poor wanderer with shelter –
> when you see the naked, to clothe them . . . ?
> (Isaiah 58.6–7)

In fact, the root of Hebrew words for generosity and justice are exactly the same, *tzedek* being commonly interpreted as 'justice', and *tzedakah* as 'generosity of charity'. Keller goes on to comment insightfully:

do justice when we give all human beings their due as creations of God. Doing justice includes not only the righting of wrongs, but generosity and social concern, especially toward the poor and vulnerable. This kind of life reflects the character of God. It consists of a broad range of dealings with people in daily life, to regular, radically generous giving of your time and resources, to activism that seeks to end particular forms of injustice, violence, and oppression.[2]

It is clear from this that a heart for justice and a desire to see the end to oppression does not absolve us from the responsibility to be generous-hearted towards those who suffer the effects of injustice now – in fact it should spur us into action in that regard.

A well-known illustration in international development is the river diagram. In this picture, the initial focus is downstream, where we see ambulances and doctors and volunteers trying desperately to lift people out of a fast-moving river and rescue them from drowning. The generosity and commitment of these volunteers and professionals is never in doubt. Their responsive action towards a crisis where lives are at risk is exemplary and must continue to happen while there are people in the river drowning.

However, we also need to ask the question, 'Why are people jumping in the river in the first place?' In the river illustration, as you pan out, further upstream is a chemical factory that is emitting toxic fumes into the air, causing people's skin to burn. That's why they are jumping in the river.

Generous justice demands that we remove the factory and its emissions *and* we save people from drowning. It's not an either/or decision.

I would go further, though, and say that the generous involvement in rescuing people from the river has the positive effect that it exposes us to the impact of injustice and causes our righteous anger to rise up and leads us to speak out and act against the systemic failures that are demanding our generosity.

Is a lack of generosity a cause of injustice?

We've seen that injustice can require us to be generous, but is a lack of generosity a cause of injustice, and in what way?

We've seen above that the owners of the chemical factory were the perpetrators of evil and oppression. There are so many things wrong about the building of the factory in the first place, but surely one of them is greed. Greed that puts the economic benefit above the safety of the community, greed that takes scarce resources and then creates pollutants that ultimately ruin creation that we were given in solemn trust to steward. Greed that is the exact opposite of generosity.

Greed that maybe wasn't generous enough to include all voices in the safe design of the factory?

Greed that maybe wasn't generous enough to collaborate with neighbours and community to determine the potential impact?

Greed that maybe wasn't generous enough to spend time and resources finding a better way?

So how, as leaders, do we develop a posture of generosity? A generosity that is inclusive and collaborative and comes from a place of abundance.

Generous inclusivity

It's good for you to invite me to the table, but it is much better for you to invite me to the kitchen.
Ghanaian proverb

Whether it is more representation on Boards, diversity in the workplace or having your voice heard in Parliament, having a seat at the table has long been the clarion call of many justice movements, and rightly so. However, a generous justice agenda needs to go much further than this. You see, the problem with 'giving people a seat at the table' is that we still see it as *our* table. Welcome to *our* table to sit at it and eat *our* food that *we* have designed, *we* have created, *we* have cooked.

Instead, generous justice requires an invitation into the kitchen. To dream and think about what ingredients we might use, what flavours and spices might add a richness to what we eat together. Co-creation is the watchword here and co-creation requires risk and courage. It also means doing the washing up together!

It's been my delight over many years to have friends who have not only invited us to dinner, but who have modelled for us an open kitchen. Food preparation is shared – and fun – and messy – as is the eating of it and the clearing up.

One thing that this signals very powerfully is the willingness to give up power, control and privilege, which in turn requires a willingness to change direction, try something different and see the world through other people's eyes.

It requires the willingness to change and to be changed. Tackling injustice with generosity will cause systems to be changed and chains to be broken – and some of those chains will be the chains that bind us. Chains of narcissism and greed, chains of unconscious bias and narrow-mindedness.

Generous posture

Adam Grant, the American Organizational Psychologist, outlines the differences of approach of those he names 'givers', 'matchers' and 'takers' in his book *Give and Take*. Professionally, he says that most of us are 'matchers' – believing work to be a zero-sum game where we are sceptical of 'takers' and afraid to make ourselves vulnerable by giving. Interestingly in this context of thinking about justice, Grant says:

> This is what I find most magnetic about successful givers: they get to the top without cutting others down, finding ways of expanding the pie that benefit themselves and the people around them. Whereas success is zero-sum in a group of takers, in groups of givers, it may be true that the whole is greater than the sum of the parts. As Simon Sinek writes, 'Givers advance the world. Takers advance themselves and hold the world back.'[3]

Grant helpfully goes on to argue that 'givers' need to distinguish generosity from three postures commonly associated with it – timidity, availability and empathy.[4] Instead, he suggests that timidity does not need to be replaced with assertiveness but by courage and agency, availability with focused giving, and empathy with empathy coupled with perspective.

Let's take each of those postures in turn and examine them more closely.

1 **Courage and agency** A generous justice is not just about giving and letting other people take but, rather, also about a posture of giving combined with courage and agency. Courage not just to give because we are being asked, but because we believe that it's the right thing to do. Courage to make the first generous move. Courage to be vulnerable and to give on behalf of others. Courage to be an agent for change – for those who can't possibly do it for themselves. Generosity, therefore, is not timid but bold, creating a new culture, cutting across the status quo and vulnerably putting ourselves in the place of victims, survivors and the marginalized.

2 **Focus** A generous justice is not just about giving randomly but also about giving in a focused way. Understanding the causes that we care about and focusing our energy in a single-minded and targeted way to make the changes happen. It is all too easy for generosity to become scattergunned in its approach and not to ask the 'why' questions. Saying no and putting in boundaries to our generosity doesn't make us takers but wise and generous givers. As leaders, trying to pour ourselves out to everyone and everything means that we can end up appearing stingy in the outworkings of our generosity because we haven't learned to say no, or to multiply our generosity by including others in the work of tackling injustice.

3 **Empathy and perspective** A generous justice absolutely requires empathy – the ability to see through the eyes of others, to experience their pain and to agonize with them. This is a vital skill and the hallmark of many generous people and many great leaders. 'They knew what I was feeling' or 'How could she have read my mind?' or 'They took so much time to focus on me' – all are great tributes to engaged leaders who have learned to practice 'emotional intelligence' and to enter into the lives, thoughts and emotions of others. Increased empathy should be a fundamental goal for those pursuing justice.

Grant makes the point, though, that, as leaders, we can't always dwell there; we have to gain perspective in order to practise generous justice.

This requires the ability to enter into others, feelings and emotions *and* the ability to stand back, ask great questions, understand what we and others can do and then generously pursue it.

Generosity from abundance

The truth is that many of us have taken more than we needed and left others hungry. We have taken more food, more power, more privilege, more ownership and we have lived by the rules of scarcity.

Those who live by the rules of scarcity pride themselves on what they have achieved and what they own: 'I made this, I own this . . . it's *mine*'. They believe that there is not enough to go around, not enough to share, not enough to be generous.

This has been well-observed in young children who have had a difficult childhood – one where milk or food at a very young age is scarce. Whenever they then come in contact with the availability of food, they will hoard it as if there is nothing more coming. It takes years for the brain to switch to understand that there will be food tomorrow. Many of us have yet to make that switch.

Those who live in the grace of abundance, however, fundamentally recognize that everything we have comes from God. Bob Pierce, founder of World Vision, understood this well when he chose the Dutch paraphrase of 1 Chronicles 29.14b as a key verse for the international relief and development organization: 'All that we have comes from God, and we give it out of His hand'.

This transforms our thinking from 'there's not enough to go around' to 'I can share'. From 'reluctant to collaborate' to 'vibrant partnership'. From 'promoting self' to 'promoting others' and from 'micromanaging' to 'openness and trust'. Ultimately, generosity and seeking generous justice requires a giving of ourselves – an emptying of ourselves – a 'kenosis'. It's an emptying of ourselves that is facilitated by an understanding of the abundance of God's love and mercy for us and modelled in the generous giving of himself by Jesus, 'who, being in very nature God, did not consider equality with God something to be used to his own advantage; rather, he made himself nothing' (Philippians 2.6–7a).

Tim Keller again puts it so well: 'It is the generosity of God, the freeness of his salvation that lays the foundation for the society of justice for all.'[5] As Izwe Nkosi reflected in his Lectio 365 Devotions just after the brutal, unjustified and horrific murder of George Floyd by a white police officer in Minneapolis in May 2020:

> The way of Jesus means emptying myself of power, privilege and possessions again and again for the sake of the least, the last and the lost, trusting the Lord to replenish what I relinquish and raise me up in due course.[6]

As we truly seek him who is abundant in grace and giving then we have everything that we need to be generous indeed.

Reflections

1 How can you start living out of abundance rather than scarcity?
2 Where do you need to invite people into the kitchen rather than to the table?
3 What steps could you take to develop a generous posture in your leadership?

Ultimately, the only power to which man should aspire is that which he exercises over himself.

ELIE WIESEL, HOLOCAUST SURVIVOR

10

Managing power

SIMON BARRINGTON

How do we view power?

All leaders have power – power to influence, power to control, power to transform, power to create and power to wound or power to cancel. Power to use for good and power to harm. So many of the stories we hear about the use of power are about its abuse, but it's also vitally important as we start this chapter to recognize that power used well can transform culture and lives – particularly when used on behalf of and in partnership with those who have less or no power.

People 'see' power in different ways. It can be seen as being held by actors – people or institutions – some more powerful than others. It can also be seen more as being distributed across relationships and social structures. Alternatively, power can be seen as a struggle between those that have it and those that don't, as a kind of zero-sum game.

How we view power – more negatively in terms of its ability to destroy and destruct or more positively in terms of its capacity to create and enhance – needs personal reflection on our own journeys and the impact that the use and abuse of power has had on us as individuals.

My own view has been shaped by a multitude of experiences. My inherited power – and therefore my overwhelming experience – is one of white middle-class male privilege (more of that in a moment). I have also been shaped, though, by my own experiences of being marginalized. My first memory of this was being ostracized and ridiculed by the other young people as the son of a youth group leader. My second was going to a youth camp where the majority language was Welsh and I was the only English speaker. The pain of both of those experiences was very real to me and my desire to speak on behalf of those who have no voice has its root in those experiences as well as in the Christian gospel. For me, though, these were transitory experiences, which while being real and lived experiences, did pass.

I've also had the privilege to live and walk alongside those for whom the lack of power is a daily lived reality that never goes away. Child-headed households in Southern Africa that have been ravaged by HIV and AIDS. The people of Nagorno-Karabakh – expelled from their own homeland to live in railway carriages and squalid camps in Azerbaijan. The people of Taiwan unable to determine their own future or the refugees from Syria stuck in refugee camps for years on end, stateless and unable to return home. The Christians of Kyrgyzstan who are unable to bury their dead because they are not allowed the paperwork to enable them to have land on which to create a cemetery.

Closer to home, in the UK, the stories of members of the Windrush generation have had a huge impact on me. These are the stories of people who arrived in the UK between 1948 and 1971 from Caribbean countries such as Jamaica, Trinidad and Tobago and other islands to help fill post-war UK labour shortages and who have suffered the indignity of deportation threats to their children because of a lack of paperwork.

This may be a very different view of power from your own – and if you have grown up in a marginalized group or have known the indignity of being abused, then your view of power and those in leadership with power is deeply rooted in your own experience.

In whatever way you view power, talking about it can be as sensitive and uncomfortable as any other subject I know. Without talking about it, though, we reinforce the existing power structures and fail to challenge how we and others handle the power that we have inherited, been given or gained.

Dealing with discomfort

As I write this in 2020, every white middle-class leader has rightly faced discomfort in the past few months as the Black Lives Matter movement has responded to the tragic and totally barbaric murder of George Floyd in Minnesota. I personally have been confronted with my own unconscious bias in a new and deeper way and had to delve deep in starting to repent of previous lack of action on behalf of the black community, who have suffered intolerable and inexcusable racist abuse, violence and exclusion.

So challenging has this experience been that Justin and I considered if having the voices of two white middle-aged men on this particular topic was now a worthwhile project at all and whether or not we would be able to write on the subject of justice, coming at it from one mono-ethnic, mono-cultural perspective. We challenged ourselves on this, considered restarting the project and listened to many friends from diverse backgrounds to determine a way forward. Ultimately, we decided that we can use our power for good to promote a debate among our peers on how much further and how much more we all need to reflect on the ways we have been shaped and are shaping society. We can't begin to encompass or embody the pain that other groups rightly feel, but we can be a good ally and a positive challenge to ourselves and our peers.

Talking about power, particularly our own, is deeply uncomfortable and is an incredibly sensitive subject to begin to address. It feels threatening to our own power or ideas about society and leadership. This has often led to resistance in the majority and an unwillingness to even discuss it.

Moving on from this requires courage, deep personal reflection and individual change – as well as creating spaces that are safe and allow us to reflect with others and to hear challenging voices – and then to go and speak of those voices to others. Doing this may require facilitation and the ability to handle emotions, conflicts and discomfort constructively. Dealing with our own discomfort, though, can be a very powerful way to see the very change that we desire come about.

Making power more visible

One of the massive challenges that we face as leaders is making power more visible – and that starts by naming it.

There is great agency in understanding our own power in a given context and therefore being more conscious of it ourselves. Imagine having a visual indicator of the level of power we have in a given situational context on our arm – or our forehead! How would that change the way we approach relationships and how would it make us more conscious of the power we possess ourselves? Would we be more conscious of our language, more conscious of our body posture, more conscious of our insensitivities to others and the things that we take for granted – such as access and opportunity?

So many times, I have found myself unconscious of the power that I have in my relationships by virtue of position, by the nature of the privilege I possess. It takes a while, for instance, to become used to the power you have as a CEO, just by nature of the title and position. Power to hire – and fire. Power to direct, power to decide, power to choose, power to bless and to curse. I discovered far too many times the power I had to affect the emotions of those I was working with – to bring about tears or smiles, laughs or anger.

A question I have used over the years to make power more visible is this: 'How would I be feeling right now in their place?' But we need to go even further than that and ask: 'What can I do in this situation to enable the forces of power at work to be exposed – to make them more visible?'

Exposing the forces of power at work

We want to see power made more visible and to get the dialogue about power out on the table – as giving permission for people to talk about power is an essential part of tackling injustice. Therefore, we need to expose the forces of power at work in a given situation – the positional power, the privilege power, the institutional power and what we call 'the power within'.

1 **Positional power** This element measures the level of power that you have because of your position. This includes power over people and resources, together with power to decide, implement and direct and the power you have through collaborations and relationships with others. These powers are normally given in, for example, schemes of delegation, job descriptions and committee or board memberships. There has been a significant move in recent years to make all of this information more transparent and open – a move that we applaud and we encourage such power to be declared and visible in all situations.

2 **Privilege** This element determines the level of power that you have because of your upbringing, your position in society, your acceptability to the prevailing culture and your leverage over other powerful people. This can be because of your race, your resources, your education, your access or your network. Moves to expose conflicts of interest and the access and influence you have are positive developments in this regard, as are paper sifts for jobs that remove race information, gender and age information. However, we must go further in exposing and challenging situations where privilege gives choices that others don't have – particularly when we are thinking about how privilege can be used to cover up abuses and hide them. Misuse of social class, educational or academic background, elitism, power-based tribalism (the 'old boys' network') and nepotism need to be challenged in every walk of life – and especially in Church life.

3 **The institutionalization of power** Of course, power is not only individual in nature and can become even more dangerous – and potentially positive – when it becomes institutionalized.

The Church as an institution shares in the problems of all institutions. The traditional problem of institutions is the abuse of power, and the Church, alongside other Christian faith-based foundations, has not been immune from this.

The French philosopher Michel Foucault argued that relationships of power are present and inevitable in all social relationships.[1] As soon as we set up systems and processes, power is present and embodied in those systems. Whether it be a committee to decide on the future direction of an organization, a safeguarding board, or simply a manager appraising an employee. The choices are always ones of fighting the system or going with it.

When a decision made by the system goes against us, there is anger with the loss of control that we feel and the inevitable mental health challenges inherent in dealing with such injustice. Just take the example of the A level results in the UK in 2020. Due to the COVID-19 pandemic, A level students were unable to take their final exams. Therefore, students had their coursework and progress assessed by their teachers and their predicted grades entered into the 'system'. The system then ran an algorithm that 'levelled' the grades to take account of previous results from their school and other factors. When the results were released, the algorithm was shown to have disadvantaged those from poorer backgrounds and enhanced the results of those from privileged backgrounds. This led to an outcry against the system and the algorithm – together with the Government that had allowed it – and the results were overturned and reset to the teacher-assessed grades.

The lack of accountability arises exactly because there is an unequal power relationship. Institutionalized power – having an impact on the lives of thousands of students – with little or no redress – is exactly the problem.

Significant parental and teacher energy and effort was invested in resolving the impact of this situation on the lives of students. In these circumstances, it is necessary to come alongside and walk with those who have suffered the injustices associated with the application of institutionalized power (as we discuss in the chapters focusing on victims and survivors).

We have to deal with the impact of the individual nature of the power we possess, but we must also deal with the systemized power and the impact it has on thousands of lives every day. We can and must do better than this.

4 **The power within** The final element we call 'the power within' is a gauge of your own self-awareness, the empathy we have for other people and our learning posture. It is a measure of our own sense of self-identity and our ability to handle power in a way that can create and empower.

It is the key to the redemption and reformation of positional, privilege and institutional power.

There is a reality that the combination of positional power *and* privilege power *and* institutional power can be multiplied together to create huge cultural and societal benefit *or*, at the other end of the spectrum, huge cultural and societal harm.

What makes the difference between these two opposite ends of the spectrum? We would argue that it is not the elimination of positional, privilege and institutional power but, rather, the redemption and reformation of them. Otherwise we just end up replacing one person's privilege with another's, one broken person's positional power with another's and replacing one broken institutional design with another. Rather, we need a reformation of the heart. A relentless focus in our development of leaders on the formation and testing of them.

In order to be exposing where all these forces of power are at work, we need to be focusing all of our leadership development effort on:

- increasing self-awareness;
- developing security in leaders' own identity;
- increasing social awareness;
- increasing cognitive, emotional and compassionate empathy.

We need to be testing our leaders on their ability to use their power to create societal good and to create cultures in which everyone flourishes. We need to be asking the questions as to whether or not, under this person's leadership, there is:

- a mutual thriving of individuals from all backgrounds;
- a culture of mutual respect;
- an environment in which all voices are heard and valued;
- an environment in which privilege is challenged;
- an environment in which there is no manipulation or coercion;
- an environment in which great social and cultural good is created and valued.

The exercise of power

So how do we exercise the power that we have – positional, privilege, institutional and the power within – for the maximum good of society and our fellow human beings? How do we exercise it to bring about justice?

Our traditional ideas of exercising power consist mainly of models of having 'power over' people. It is helpful to move away from this model to a model that thinks about having 'power with', 'power to' and that is 'empowering'.[2]

Power over . . .

Our models of power tend towards thinking about domination and have many negative associations – repression, force, manipulation, coercion and abuse. 'Having power involves taking it from someone else, and then using it to dominate and prevent others from gaining it.'[3]

Our models of having 'power over' perpetuate and drive continuing inequality, injustice, poverty and oppression. They paint the picture of a constant power struggle where the oppressed becomes the oppressor who then exercises power over the newly oppressed. You either have power or you are subject to it and you must fight for what you can get. You are the victim or the perpetrator, those with or those without.

Sadly, it is our observation that years of being marginalized do not automatically prepare you to lead with equity and inclusion, or to use power well. Instead, new models of leadership are required that teach us to use power well.

In recent years, models of empowerment in international development have sought to challenge this thinking. Models that talk about 'power with', 'power to' and 'empowerment' have become increasingly powerful in communities that have been ravaged by poverty and disaster and that have their own inbuilt inequities – for instance towards women and girls – that need challenging and changing.

Power with . . .

A sense of the whole being greater than the sum of the individuals, especially when a group tackles problems together.[4]

This is all about finding common ground among different participants and building networks and movements that build collective strength. Think of current examples such as Extinction Rebellion, or past examples such as 'Make Poverty History' or the 'Keep Sunday Special' campaign – which was an alignment of trade unions and religious groups who found a powerful voice together on an issue – even though they disagreed on much else.

'Power with' is based on mutual support, solidarity and collaboration and brings together and magnifies the individual strengths, information, skills and knowledge to tackle a common problem. In many ways we are seeking to be 'power with' groups as diverse as #MeToo and gender equality groups in being an ally with them for the causes they are championing and contributing our voice to theirs – albeit from a different perspective.

Power to . . .

This refers to the unique potential power that each individual has to make a difference. Witness Greta Thunberg and the simple, yet prophetic act of a school strike, together with a clear articulation of the issues that turned a nine-year-old girl into the catalyst for a global movement to tackle climate change.

As leaders, we must believe in and exercise power that builds up individuals and enables them to recognize the unique skills and attributes that they have. We must be able to see the huge unique potential in each person, not as a threat to our own insecurity, but as a possibility for change and development.

A belief and investment in equal education and access for all, and the willingness to invest in individuals and enable them to reach their goals – regardless of their background – are critical in our fight against injustice.

Empowering

Empowerment in its simplest definition is 'bringing people outside the decision-making process into it'.[5] This is very much focused, though, on giving 'power to'. However, it is vital as we seek to empower victims, the marginalized and those without privilege to enable them to have an equal place in the kitchen for co-creating a more just leadership and just society.

We must go further and as Jo Rowlands says:

Within the generative, 'power to' and 'power with', interpretation of power, empowerment is concerned with the processes by which people become aware of their own interests and how those relate to the interests of others, in order both to participate from a position of greater strength in decision-making and actually to influence such decisions.

Rowlands goes on to articulate that, if as leaders we really want to empower, we must focus on three specific aspects of empowerment:

1 **personal** building up individuals' self-respect, identity and confidence to enable them to contribute fully;
2 **relational** building up the capacity to form effective relationships that work collaboratively together;
3 **collective** building up the capacity for groups to work together, advocate, lobby and address local, national and international issues.

Ultimately, we must strive for the vision that Blaise Pascal so beautifully articulated: 'Justice and Power must be brought together, so that whatever is just may be powerful, and whatever is powerful may be just.'[6]

Reflections

1 Who can you have a conversation with about the power that you hold – positional, privilege, institutional – and how well you are handling that power?
2 What can you do to take steps to make power more visible in your organization?
3 How can you develop your own self-awareness, empathy and ability to handle power well?

Have I not commanded you? Be strong and courageous. Do not be afraid; do not be discouraged, for the Lord your God will be with you wherever you go.

(JOSHUA 1.9)

11

Being courageous

JUSTIN HUMPHREYS

The words in the book of Joshua are so powerful, aren't they? I recall this short passage being one of those that I learned as a young boy in Sunday school class all those years ago. If these words are not the epitome of encouragement, I don't know which would be.

'Lord, help me get one more!'

Among the many tales of courage you can think of, you might be familiar with the incredible story of Desmond Doss. For those who don't recognize his name, he was the conscientious objector and combat medic portrayed in the Second World War film *Hacksaw Ridge*.[1] This has got to be one of my all-time favourites. It makes for a tense and, at times, gory watch, but it tells of the most unparalleled courage. One man, armed only with his faith and courage, saved more than seventy-five wounded soldiers from almost certain death following a bloody and prolonged engagement with the enemy on Okinawa Island.

In her biographical account of her husband's exploits, his second wife, Frances Doss, recounts that Desmond (a devout Seventh Day Adventist) had no awareness of how many men he had rescued that day until his superior officers gave him their estimate. He simply kept going back time after time into the hell in front of him, praying 'Lord, help me get one more!'[2] That's immense courage without question.

Where does such courage come from and what can we as leaders learn from it in our pursuit of justice? Gary Haugen, the President and CEO of the International Justice Mission, suggests that we all have an inner yearning to be brave (to exercise courage) that is a natural, God-given gift and instinctive drive:

> Why is it so beautiful to see someone do the right thing when it is hard? Why, on the other hand, should there be such shame about our cowardice? Why should it matter so much to my inner being that I do the right thing rather than the safe thing? It's a mystery. But there it is, pointing relentlessly to the nature and delight of the One who made me.[3]

This idea places the desire to do the right thing (for someone else) and the realization that we may not be safe in pursuing the thing that is in front of us in direct conflict with each other. It appears to me that there are at least two key factors in this suggested premise. First, that we have the ability to put a greater value on the life or experience of another person above our own. Second, that we are prepared to face our fear of the unknown – that may present some form of danger to us – and step out into that unknown. Selflessness is at the core of this approach – it is a quality or characteristic that is not so common in leadership these days. Not at least in the aspects of life where it might make a tangible difference to others. This ability to put others first or above ourselves requires an acute and relentless acceptance that we are of no greater worth than anyone else. That is not to diminish our own value, but to know that each and every human being is of infinite and equal value and made in the image of God: 'So, God created mankind in his own image, in the image of God he created them; male and female he created them' (Genesis 1.27).

The second part of this idea of what it takes to have courage is that we are prepared to face our fears. Whether we are fearful of speaking in front of large numbers of people or small groups of people; fearful of competition or fearful of conflict of any kind; the willingness to forge ahead and rise above regardless is what edges us towards our goal with courage.

Confidence or courage?

Clearly, these are only a couple of brief reflections on what it takes to be courageous. There is obviously much more to developing our pathways to courage than that! One aspect of this that has struck me is whether it is confidence that feeds courage or vice versa. I am certain that one cannot exist without the other, but which comes first? Maybe it's not that helpful to try and work this out. There are probably just as many arguments in favour of one suggestion as the other. The important thing to understand is that they essentially exist within a self-generating, symbiotic cycle if you like (see Figure 4). That is to say that one cannot exist without the other and one plays no greater part in the end result than the other.

Do you remember when you were in primary school and sports day would include the three-legged race? It's a powerful analogy when applied in this context. Two people, hopefully of equal strength if not equal desire to win, would be connected by tying their neighbouring legs together, thus creating a three-legged running machine. The power was actually in the fact that the two individuals would both be running as hard as they could (hopefully in synchronized fashion), harnessing the power brought by both runners. If one runner faltered, the other runner would also falter; synchronization would be lost and the race forfeited. So it is, I suggest, with courage and confidence: one generates the other and each sustains the other.

There may be multiple factors that you could cite that have assisted you to feel either confident or courageous in the face of challenging or unfamiliar circumstances. And there it is, unfamiliarity. The development of familiarity by definition can only be achieved by repeated exposure to

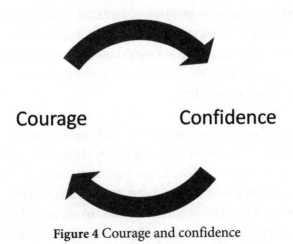

Courage   **Confidence**

Figure 4 Courage and confidence

that thing or situation. Once we have become familiar with something or someone, our confidence rises and our courage with it. But we must be careful not to let this familiarity exceed its usefulness. The old adage 'familiarity breeds contempt' is a cautionary one that suggests once we have become too familiar, our respect for that person or situation diminishes and negative consequences can be felt. The result of which can be arrogance, conceit and false confidence. As ever, our ability to be self-reflective and self-regulating in this regard will help us to walk this fine line – or at least stay the right side of it.

Fear and humility

In the analogy of the three-legged race, it was hopefully clear to see what happens when the two people run in synergy with each other. But what happens when one or other of them loses that sense of pace and why might this happen? The 'f word' is often the culprit – I mean fear. Before we go any further in this section, I want to address the very existence of fear as something that is experienced by leaders in all contexts. One of the characteristics of safer, healthier leadership is the ability to exercise humility and admit when we are fearful or that we don't know all the answers. Fear, and especially the fear of failure, is not necessarily a bad thing. What's important is the way we handle it and relate to others in the process:

> There is great power in a position of humility and correction taken by a church leader . . . for survivors [of church-based abuse] to know that there is acceptance and acknowledgement of such failings will go a long way to healing the wounds and building firmer foundations for change going forward.[4]

This exercise in humility to counter fear and shame is not only necessary when facing our own failures. Facing our fears with humility is just as necessary when confronted with the reality of the task ahead of us to find or restore justice where it has been denied or robbed by others. Let's take the story of Moses to illustrate a point. In chapter three of Exodus, we read the story of Moses meeting God in the form of the burning bush.

Early in that conversation, God asks Moses to go and deliver a difficult message to the King of Egypt:

> 'So now, go. I am sending you to Pharaoh to bring my people the Israelites out of Egypt.' But Moses said to God, 'Who am I that I should go to Pharaoh and bring the Israelites out of Egypt?' And God said, 'I will be with you.'
> (Exodus 3.10–12)

So Moses' fear, or at least a lack of courage or confidence, is met by God giving him everything he needs. God says, 'I will be with you'. Does this satisfy Moses? Well, let's read on. There is much further discussion about God's instructions and the clarity that Moses would need to engage Pharaoh with this difficult message. Ultimately, Moses remains unconvinced in his own abilities and fails to see how God could assist him: 'Moses said to the Lord, "Pardon your servant, Lord. I have never been eloquent, neither in the past nor since you have spoken to your servant. I am slow of speech and tongue"' (Exodus 4.10).

Right, so Moses was not a gifted speaker it would appear. Not only is he owning this reality, but it is almost as if he is denying God's ability to change it ('neither in the past nor since you have spoken'). We may think, wow, that's short-sighted. But isn't this something that we could all imagine saying to God at some point? We might say, 'This is too hard', or, 'That's too hard', or, 'I can't do this or that' ('. . . and I lack faith that you can do anything to change it').

The problem that Moses faced is probably a very common fear for many leaders to this day. Despite God's clear irritation with Moses a little later in this passage, we don't read of Moses being sacked from his position as leader of the Israelites. He continued, albeit without entering the promised land until his death, after which his protégé Joshua took over. Moses did go to speak to Pharaoh with his brother Aaron at his side – a man who was apparently more eloquent than Moses. Together they issued that now famous instruction to Pharaoh: 'Let my people go!' But it was still Moses through whom God showed himself to Pharaoh – remember under God's instruction, Moses issues a command to Aaron to throw down his staff for it to turn into a snake as a show of God's power.

The message here is that, as leaders, we are all likely to be confronted with our own fear at times of challenge. This will certainly be the case as we lead the fight against injustice in whatever sphere we are working. The key is to acknowledge that fear, understand where it comes from and harness our energies to fix our eyes on the goal. Alongside this, as in the story of Moses and Pharaoh, we mustn't fall into the trap of thinking we are the only ones who alone can bring change – that would be arrogant. We must recognize our own limitations (and the strengths of others) and work together to maximize the collective skills and expertise that can be brought to the fight. After all, wasn't this the experience of Moses when God provided him with his brother to help him deal with that impossible mission of speaking to Pharaoh?

Facing fears and finding strength

This may seem an obvious point but, provided we are prepared to face our fears and work through them, we will hopefully find new strength. New strength to not only deal with the challenges we have previously encountered, but also to confront new challenges when they emerge and maybe even have some capacity to anticipate them before they occur. But how might we do this constructively? After all, we cannot predict with any real certainty what tomorrow will bring, let alone what next week or next year might bring. We know this more than ever just now. As I am writing this, the UK has emerged from the 'first wave' of the global COVID-19 pandemic and is just realizing that the 'second wave' has already arrived and begun to gather momentum. Forward planning and anticipating the future is very hard in these days.

Returning to the world of sport again for a moment, we can learn from research into sport science and physiotherapy methods that the manner in which our muscles are conditioned and strengthened plays a huge part in overall performance. In this discipline, sports therapists and athletes understand the concept of 'range of motion' (ROM).[5] This is the degree to which a joint moves in physical exercise. A lack of exercise will, as you would expect, result in a lower ROM – the joint and its related muscles are out of practice and the elasticity (or range) is reduced. Conversely, a well-exercised joint will enjoy a greater range of movement.

Returning to the question of how we develop strength in facing our fears constructively, there is much to transfer from this area of physiotherapy. Range of motion (or, let's say, confidence and courage) can be developed in two primary ways: active technique and passive technique. Active technique would involve us identifying areas of resistance or muscle weakness and proactively undertaking exercises specifically to address these (for example running or resistance training, such as lifting weights). Passive technique would involve another person undertaking these exercises for us, particularly when a trauma, nerve damage or illness has incapacitated us. This technique will only maintain flexibility, but has less impact on developing overall strength as less resistance can be applied.

Have you ever wondered why you see runners doing all those weird stretching movements up against a wall or on their front drive before they embark on the morning run? They are undertaking active techniques to improve the range of motion of the key muscles and joints in the legs and feet in anticipation of the work they are about to do. It's as if they are saying to their bodies, 'Come on, wake up, you're about to experience some challenge so let's get ready'. It's where the expression 'limbering-up' comes from. Knowing the right amount of stretching and other methods you should use will very much depend on what you are facing (i.e. mild, medium or severe challenge) and whether you are needing to avoid injury or build longer-term stamina.[6]

Can we transfer this analogy helpfully to facing our fears? I think we can. If we take range of motion to be confidence or courage levels, the same principles can be applied. Adopting both timely and active exercise (limbering-up or building our level of confidence and courage) we will give ourselves the best chance for gaining strength in areas of potential weakness. Almost in the same way as we 'keep short accounts' – we deal with things as they appear, so that they do not gather momentum and have an impact beyond a tolerable level. As I have said before, working towards justice and with justice is not easy. It requires practice, patience and a positive attitude towards challenge.

It's not all about you!

Have you seen the 2006 film *Facing the Giants*? Through the story of a high school American football team, we see that being the underdogs is a scenario in which God can move mightily in us and through us. Yes, this told the story of ultimate success for the football team and its coach, but more than that it tells us that in hopeless scenarios, God can still be victorious if we let him play a part.

In the story, Coach Grant, who had been failing to make the grade for six successive seasons, finally turned to God and faced his ultimate fear – that he wasn't good enough. He faced the facts (repeated failure over six seasons and having just lost his star player to another school) and sought God's guidance about how to turn things around. In that act, the power of his fears was broken. The facts didn't disappear or get erased like some magical swipe across a school whiteboard. They were still the facts, but Coach Grant's view of them changed. They were put into a new perspective, relative to who he had just enlisted to help him.

This is all good and should motivate us to consider how we might approach our own fears and past failures as we try our hardest to be courageous. But at the end of all this, we need to acknowledge that it's not about you! It's about him. How are we bringing glory to God in our trials and troubles? Are we letting him take control? Essentially, are we abandoning ourselves to his perfect way? Seeking justice for those who have been wronged is one of the most powerful ways for us to play our part in what I believe is one of God's top priorities for us on earth. The words of the prophet Micah, that we all know well, bring this into sharp focus for us: 'He has shown you, O mortal, what is good. And what does the LORD require of you? To act justly and to love mercy and to walk humbly with your God' (Micah 6.8).

As you're reading this book, I would imagine that you might agree that acting justly and loving mercy are undoubtedly two of the most important ingredients for us as we live out our Christian faith. But what about walking humbly with God? I believe (from my own personal experience) that this is perhaps the most difficult part of this tripartite instruction. It means that we must think less of ourselves and more of him (and those we are serving). We must allow God to be in control, so that in our pursuit of those things that please him (such as justice and mercy), we have an opportunity to bring glory to him. So, when all is said and done, it's helpful to be reminded that it's not all about you – it's all about God!

Reflections

1 Where do you need to limber up and get ready to face your fears?
2 Where are you deeply challenged and need a total dependence on God for the courage and confidence you will need to lead?
3 How are you bringing glory to God in the most difficult circumstances you are facing?

JUST LEADERSHIP:
ACTION

Our lives succeed or fail gradually, then suddenly, one conversation at a time.

KEN BLANCHARD[1]

12

Tackling the difficult stuff

SIMON BARRINGTON

No matter the issue of injustice we are tackling as leaders, ultimately, it will come down to our willingness to have the difficult conversations, to exercise responsibility and to put our courage and confidence into action. To overcome our fears and to 'dare greatly'[2] and enter into the arena where our convictions about justice can be tested. To tackle the difficult stuff.

We can have all the right motives, all the right attitudes, all the right convictions, but will we speak out or will we remain silent? Will we step up or sit back?

Have we the emotional energy to face the ensuing conflict, or is it just easier for everyone to opt for the polite and inane response and just hope the situation goes away?

You know the scenario. However inexperienced a leader you are, you've already faced it many times. You can see that a situation is developing in your workplace in front of your eyes. One person has been treated unjustly, in your view, and your blood is boiling. Maybe your colleague has been passed over for a promotion, been the victim of racism, been ridiculed unfairly by a colleague, been the butt of an office joke or suffered harassment or abuse.

Your desire to act justly, love mercy and walk humbly with God is rising strong within you and you are considering your approach. How do you even start to tackle this? What can be done? Do you have a right to speak up? What will the consequences be and what might it mean for your career?

This is the moment of truth. To let things lie or to stand up?

Often, we stall at this point because we play out the whole scenario in our minds rather than focus on the reality of the present moment. We ask the 'What if?' questions and our brain's scenario-planning functions go into overdrive and we become paralysed by the myriad possible outcomes – most of which will never occur. But what if tackling injustice just began with the next conversation you do or don't have? What if it was possible that the next conversation could change the trajectory of your leadership and the life of your colleague?

Having the difficult conversations

Susan Scott, in her brilliant book, *Fierce Conversations: Achieving success in work and in life, one conversation at a time,* puts it wonderfully and with force:

> Take your finger and touch your nose. This is where the resolution begins. This is the accountable position. If you want to make progress towards a better 'here' in your professional or personal life, identify the conversations out there with your name on them and resolve to have them with all the courage, grace, and vulnerability they require.[3]

She continues: 'A fierce conversation is one in which we come out from behind ourselves into the conversation and make it real.'

But why do we find this so difficult? Why is this the moment that we find ourselves procrastinating and so unsure of ourselves and our convictions? Why is this so hard?

Brené Brown argues that it is because this is the moment that we need to learn to become vulnerable. That our courage, our willingness to step out, exposes something deep inside us that is raw and fragile and speaks to our hearts and our identity.

> In those moments, we need to stop and breathe – bring clarity and awareness to what we are trying to avoid – then get clear about what needs to be done and step into vulnerability. When we find ourselves zigzagging – hiding out, pretending, avoiding, procrastinating, rationalising, blaming, lying – we need to remind ourselves that running is a huge energy suck and probably way outside our values. At some point we have to turn towards vulnerability and make that call.[4]

For us as Christians, it's a moment for prayerful reflection. A moment to cry out to our Father for strength, humility and courage. A moment to find God's strength in our weakness. A moment when we ask the author of justice to empower us to tackle the injustice that is a mark of sin – individual or systemic – and to then step boldly into the next conversation.

What makes the difference between being a leader or not is how you respond in the moment.[5]

Principles of difficult conversations

1 **Have the conversation early** The Advisory, Conciliation and Arbitration Service (ACAS) in its policy paper 'Fairness, justice and capability: Repositioning conflict management' emphasizes the importance of early interventions and an environment of fairness that encourages them:

   managers who are able to listen, negotiate and influence are more likely to both enhance voice and organisational justice by creating a culture in which employees feel able to express their concerns and in which staff feel confident that problems will be managed fairly. By having quality conversations, it is more likely that performance issues will be addressed and any conflict between staff will be resolved at an early stage. This will not only mean improved performance but fewer disputes and a greater likelihood of positive working relationships.[6]

2 **Make it real** Difficult conversations need to be real conversations. No skirting around the issues. No emotive descriptions. Just the plain, real facts. If we are serious about tackling injustice, then we have to get the reality from our perspective on the table. As you prepare, question that reality like a barrister would in a court of law. What stands up to scrutiny, what don't you know, what questions do you have yourself?

3 **Be emotionally prepared** In understanding our reality, we must also be committed to understanding how our emotions are affecting that view of reality. We must take responsibility for being self-aware and socially aware and learn to deliver difficult realities without emotional baggage, but instead with clarity, conviction and passion.

4 **Be prepared to listen ruthlessly** Reality is complex – the world is complex. In getting your reality on the table then you need to be

prepared to listen to reality from the other person's perspective. You may be viewing the earth from the moon, but they may be viewing it from Venus – or from another galaxy!

5 **Be fully present** Develop the capability to be fully present in the conversation as if this conversation is the only one that ever mattered and as if this conversation can change the whole world and change your world. Maybe, just maybe, it could?

6 **Create safety for the other party and be on the lookout for your own defensiveness** Ask yourself the questions – what would make it safer for the other person and where am I likely to get defensive?

7 **Be prepared that this conversation is only the start** Any conversation has the possibility of resolution, but most likely it will only be the start. It will only be the start of the transformation of the situation, but it will be a start. Don't expect the final outcome from a first conversation. An offer of further dialogue is a result. An offer of going away to think about it is a result.

8 **Let silence happen** Lack of words does not indicate something meaningful is not taking place. We typically want to rush in and fill the silent gaps, but in these spaces, we often overlook the meaningful and replace it with meaningless. The times of quiet are invaluable and in themselves often convey so much.

9 **Be prepared for conflict** Whereas concerns for justice are universal, views of what is just and what is unjust are not universally shared. Your difficult conversation, therefore, may lead you into a conflict situation and a series of further conversations and actions. Understanding conflict, and becoming adept at managing and addressing it, is a vital role of a just leader.

So how do we do conflict justly?

Just conflict

Conflict is inevitable if we are to lead justly. We cannot pretend to stand up to systemic and individual injustice without recognizing the spiritual forces at work behind them. We cannot approach conflict without recognizing the spiritual work that we are engaged in.

We can't stand up to the scar of racism without the power of the cross. We can't stand up to the tragedy of slavery without an understanding of the evil of greed and exploitation behind it. It's no wonder we see conflict as difficult, but we must dispel the Christian myth that all conflict is bad.

Sandra Cobbin, in her Grove booklet 'Leadership resilience in conflict', argues that conflict is often seen as a distraction, frustrating and embarrassing and that our theology of conflict does not enable us to see the opportunities for transformation that conflict gives us. 'In the darkness, brokenness and messiness of conflict there is the opportunity to discover God's creativity, reconciliation and grace at work.'[7] In facing up to conflict we have the opportunity to see justice arriving, to see the Kingdom arriving, to see the gospel at work in the reconciling of all things.

Cobbin continues:

Ultimately the Bible is a story about God's transforming grace, which weaves its way like a golden thread through stories of hatred, murder, lies and deceit. The conflict between King David, Uriah and Bathsheba is transformed by God's thread of grace, which brings Solomon to the throne. The conflict between Sarah and Hagar is transformed by God's thread of grace, as God meets with Hagar and blesses her son Ishmael with many descendants. Situations of conflict rarely become neat and tidy as a result of God's grace-move. Instead, amidst the messiness a new future opens up, shaped by the conflict, but no longer defined by it. It is a future in which there is new life and light, made possible by God's transforming grace.[8]

Conflict transformation

It's helpful to think about conflict therefore as more about transformation than about resolution. We may never see the resolution of all injustice in our lifetime, but we can see transformation. We may not see the elimination of slavery, racism and abuse in our lifetime, but we can see transformation in all of those situations.

When we see conflict as aiming for transformation, we see our primary role as participating in the redemptive and reconciling work of the gospel and conflict no longer seems divisive or a distraction, even though it is rarely painless but, rather, kingdom work.

Leading through conflict

In the Forge Leadership research into millennials as leaders that we conducted in 2018, millennial leaders identified leading through conflict as the single most difficult issue facing them in the workplace. And yet less than a third of the leaders had had any training in conflict management in their organization.

This is not the place to take you through a detailed approach to conflict management with all its intricacies and challenges. However, as you are serious about tackling injustice, we would encourage you to invest in getting training on conflict transformation and would highly recommend the course 'Transforming Conflict' from Bridge Builders Ministries as a core foundational course in this area.[9]

Similarly, the conflict resolution models from Speed B. Leas of the Alban Institute are foundational in understanding the different levels of conflict: (1) problem to solve; (2) disagreement; (3) contest; (4) fight or flight; (5) intractable situations and the different goals, behaviours, language, group make-up and, critically, the type of intervention needed to bring resolution.[10]

The emotional side of conflict

Leaders tend to respond to conflict by either remaining emotionally removed from the situation and taking an academic approach, or by becoming emotionally entangled with the situation in an unhealthy way.

An emotionally removed posture is generally driven by our logical thinking. This may be because we have been wounded before in a similar situation or are not used to engaging with our emotions and we would rather supress them than face the danger of them causing us to become uncontrolled.

An emotionally entwined posture is driven by our own emotions and heart, entanglement with the emotions of others and the anxiety of the situation which we can have a tendency to absorb, often referred to as projection and transference in psychological terms.

Both extremes are unbalanced and in seeking to be just leaders we need to pursue a position of emotional balance which enables us to respond with our head and our heart – to put forward clear positions while remaining open to listen to the positions that others are holding.

In the heat of the moment in a conflict conversation, when the anxiety is high and increasing, this is easier said than done and takes time and practice in order for us to be a non-anxious presence in any situation.

Being a non-anxious presence

Edwin Friedman, the rabbi, family therapist and leadership consultant, first put forward the idea of a non-anxious presence. David Cox explains Friedman's theory:

> To the extent leaders and consultants can maintain a 'non-anxious presence' in a highly energized anxiety field, they can have the same effects on that field that transformers have in an electrical circuit. They reduce the negative energy in a field by the nature of their own presence and being, as well as by the field they, in effect, set up. This is not a matter of breaking a circuit; it requires staying in touch without getting zapped. Persons can remain non-anxious if they are not present. The trick is to be both non-anxious and present simultaneously.[11]

This requires us to be objective (or 'differentiated') and able to ask the questions about what is going on in the system, as well as to engage empathetically on behalf of those who have been hurt by the system.

Cox continues:

> A major sign of being better differentiated is when the leader can be present in the midst of emotional turmoil and actively relate to key people while calmly maintaining a sense of the leader's own direction. Developing greater clarity about what is happening in a system will always be more productive in the long run than just having empathy for the hurting people in the system and trying to rescue them.

But how do we do that in practice?

Looking after yourself in the midst of conflict

In more recent years, there has been a rise in the understanding on the imperative of leaders to keep themselves emotionally healthy and therefore to become a non-anxious presence. Pete Scazzero, John Mark Comer and John Eldredge have been key advocates on behalf of tackling the propensity for leaders to burn themselves out rapidly in ministry and the promotion of better and more sustainable rhythms of life.

If that is true generally for leaders, then how much more so for leaders who are seeking to tackle the hard stuff, who seek to tackle injustice, who throw themselves into the necessity of conflict in order to see the transformation we desire.

Particularly when we find ourselves in the midst of tackling conflict, it's necessary for us to remember to take the time to reinforce the rhythms that sustain us. Because we are likely to be more tired and more stretched than ever by the very nature of the conflict, then this requires extra effort and focus.

The following rhythms can sustain us and they can provide the foundations out of which we can become a non-anxious presence in the midst of the most challenging moments of our lives and leadership.

1 **Pursue rhythms of companionship** Taking time to be with those that we love and those that love us unconditionally can remind us of the presence of the unconditional love of God in our lives and that ultimately this is not about us. It can also remind us of our humanity and be a gift of the grace and mercy of God in our lives. The tendency to overfocus on the conflict can be dissipated by a walk in the woods, the gift of laughter from a child, the touch of a hand, a hug or the presence of a non-judgemental listening ear.

2 **Pursue rhythms of joy** What gives you life? Playing the piano, for me, or walks by the sea bring delight and joy. Pursue rhythms of joy in the darkest moments of conflict. Take time to breathe, to delight in beauty and the simple joys of life. Slow down enough to smell the coffee, breathe long enough to feel and sense the presence of God, try eating more slowly and doing things that bring you joy.

3 **Pursue rhythms of rest** Sometimes the kindest and best thing you can do to pursue justice is to go and have a long sleep! To recognize that your body as well as your mind needs to seek justice, that a saw can't always be cutting wood and remain sharp.

As Christians there is a growing appreciation of removing the hurry from our lives and particularly for practising Sabbath. It's taken me some time to get used to that idea, because my experience of the practice of it when I was growing up was one of boredom and religiosity. Increasingly, though, I am finding that the practice of switching off my phone, focusing on God, companionship and things that bring me joy for one day a week – is life-giving and liberating and restful.

4 **Pursue rhythms of prayer and reflection** Keeping close to God is ultimately the sustenance that we need. I have a saying which seems to resonate with the leaders I coach or train: 'The invitation to a deeper intimacy with Jesus is in the most intractable problem that you face today.' Or we may say, in the largest injustice you are seeking to address, in the most hideous abuse you are exposing, in the hardest relationship you are working at.

Establishing patterns that push into rather than away from the One who is reconciler of all things – Jesus Christ – reminds us of the source of the justice that we seek and without whose strength and sustaining we are simply powerless.

Reflections

1 What steps could you take to be more of a non-anxious presence in your organization?
2 Where do you need to have the courage to have that difficult conversation?
3 How can you look after yourself better when you are in the midst of conflict?

Change will not come if we wait for some other person, or if we wait for some other time. We are the ones we've been waiting for. We are the change that we seek.

BARACK OBAMA, 44TH PRESIDENT OF THE UNITED STATES OF AMERICA

13

Making change happen

JUSTIN HUMPHREYS

There is little more exciting than being a part of some great, positive change. Better still, when we know that we are partnering with God in that change because it comes from his heart for justice. Of course, change is the thing that many will resist and that many are fearful of. Strategizing and succeeding in the implementation of such positive change is no easy task either, right?

I have to tell you that there is one thing that stirs me to action more than anything else – seeing injustice. Knowing that I can and should do something about it is something over which I have almost no control. I recall one day, some years ago, being introduced by my friend and senior pastor at the time, as I was about to deliver that week's sermon. On that occasion, the introduction went something like this:

Let's welcome Justin to the platform this morning. I know he will have a great message for us. He is going to be speaking about God's justice. This might be interesting, because we all know that he has such a heart for this, that he can barely utter the word 'justice' without crying!

Break my heart for what breaks yours

What is that all about? It could be that I am just so appalled by the notion of injustice. It could be that, out of my own personal experiences (some of which I described in an earlier chapter), I feel some deep sense of empathy with others who experience injustice. It might be that, among all the great things the Bible teaches us, the constant call to justice resonates with me the most. In actual fact, I think it is all these things but, in addition, I think it is an acute awareness that this is also God's heart's cry for change. He sees injustice and it breaks his heart.

Have you ever had a time when the Spirit moves you so deeply that it feels like the frozen air has stolen your breath and you can barely speak? When your only response can be to weep? I often think of that Christian song with the line, 'Break my heart, Lord, for what breaks yours'. That, right there, is a line that you need courage to sing if you really mean it. For our hearts to break in the way God's heart breaks over injustice means that we will be unable to avoid seeing the need for change. I have often wept singing those words!

If we're honest, for those of us who have had the personal or professional task of dealing with past abuse and injustice, how many times do we find ourselves looking back at things and expending huge amounts of time and energy trying to apportion blame or point the finger at others? Wouldn't it be more productive to simply acknowledge that abuse happens in any context and culture where it is allowed to flourish, learn the lessons from past experience and apply this learning to strive for a better future?

The answer has to be yes, but in doing so, we must also be prepared to look in the mirror and consider what part we have had to play in the history or formation of any culture that may have become abusive (or at least not as safe and just as it could be). As leaders, we must take responsibility for the ways we have personally and corporately failed and be willing to take the necessary steps to shoulder that responsibility and the reparations that must come as a result. Apologies and learning lessons are important steps in the process of responding to abuse and other injustices, but too often that is where we stop. Truly taking responsibility and learning lessons means that we must be seen to make active, tangible and timely steps towards change and encourage others to do the same.

Changing the narrative

Whether you are a business leader, a charity leader or a church leader, you will be familiar with the concept of needing to 'buck the trend', 'get ahead of the curve' or 'change the narrative'. What all these phrases point towards is change, but not change for change's sake. This kind of change is led out of a recognition that what is happening cannot be allowed to continue to the detriment of the organization, its goals or even society at large. This idea in the context of church leadership in a postmodern, pluralistic society is explored by Eddie Gibbs, who clearly understands the need to be aware of past and changing culture as part of a context for shaping the future:

> Today's church leaders must be trained to observe and interpret the cultural changes taking place through society . . . If church leaders fail to respond to such changes, they are likely to lead the church into decline as they cling to outmoded ways of thinking and working.[1]

Translating this into our context of *just leadership* brings us face to face with a real challenge. Much of my time in recent years leading thirtyone:eight has been spent working with organizations that are either trying to learn lessons from abuses that have taken place or those that are attempting to prevent them from occurring in the first place. Even in these two sides of the same coin (preventative v. responsive), we see change as a catalyst at play. For those who have clear lessons to learn, possibly from high-profile abuse scandals they have faced in their organizations, they are exploring 'what was' in an effort to prevent that being 'what is' or 'what will be' in the future. For those who do not have a specific incident or scandal to learn from, they are seeking to ensure that the possibility of such things happening elsewhere are not hiding in their blind spot, ready to catch them by surprise and up end their efforts. So where might you be in all this? Are you going to engage with the possibility of injustice taking root, or will you wait until the reality is staring you in the face?

The sad reality for too many churches and organizations that we could probably all bring to mind from recent times, is that they failed to take the preventative or proactive approach. But worse than this are those churches or organizations that have failed victims and survivors not once, but on multiple occasions. Those places and their leaders, who, when brought face to face with abuses by the victims themselves, take insufficient or, even worse, no care to respond appropriately, perpetuate a narrative that shows the Church or organization in a very dim light. In Chapter 5, I talked about the effect of re-abuse that this creates.

I have no doubt about this – and I have been certain about it for some years now – that one of the greatest threats to the Church today is its continued failure to weed out the roots of unsafe and unhealthy culture and practices. It is anathema to think that our churches are not the places of safety, refuge, healing and flourishing that they are called to be. This has to change if the Church is to survive and be a true model of Christianity!

In my previous book, I explore a range of ways to map and assess safer, healthier culture in our organizations – to minimize the threat of our blind spots, if you like.[2] Part of this requires leaders to be alert to what others say about our organizational efforts to deal with and learn from past failures, abuses or injustices. This is all part of the commentary and messaging that we generate. Our ability to reflect both personally and corporately on these things is an important part of the journey to understanding where we might need to effect change.

What is being said by others is important as this can either reflect well or badly on our efforts. More importantly also, it is often our first opportunity to demonstrate to those who require a refuge or place of safety to come to us in the first place. Having a clear commitment to being justice-minded and justice-driven sends a strong message – and it starts with you as the leader! So, sometimes, there is a real need to stop and change the prevailing narrative or change the system within which it occurs (just like King Lemuel). To start to communicate and embed more positive messages that give confidence and demonstrate our ability to learn and change.

Leaving a legacy

In doing these things, there is an amazing opportunity to leave a better legacy that will become the firm foundation for the pursuit of justice within and through our churches for the next generation. This is something that will require purposeful and proactive effort. Gary Haugen describes this as 'cultivating a compassionate awareness', in which he states: 'Precisely because it is not our first or natural inclination, we are called to a conscious effort of reserving a space in our thought life for those who suffer abuse and oppression in our world.'[3]

Changing the landscape sufficiently that it is worthy of being left as fertile ground for future generations to grow and practise justice, means that as leaders we have to make the effort to first create something new. Once we have changed the narrative and begun to shape what could be, we have a responsibility to provide the next generation with the tools to keep it alive. Earlier in 2020, I spoke at The Justice Conference UK to launch our new 'Safer Places Pledge'[4] – one of the key elements of this pledge for leaders is about the need to commit to being the change that we seek in this pursuit of justice, fairness, equality and freedom from abuse.

I have been both surprised and delighted when seeing those green shoots of hope – those glimpses of what could be. I recall on one occasion preparing myself mentally and spiritually for delivering a guest lecture to a group of final-year students at a well-known theological college in London. The group were typically of a younger profile – probably exclusively millennials. Preparation is obviously always good ahead of such events, but I discovered that I had been preparing myself for something that did not occur. Rather than being met with a barrage of arguments or scepticism about the topic, I was amazed to find that the students had engaged with the subject matter in advance and had come armed with all manner of insightful and searching questions to improve their understanding. They were hungry to engage, but more importantly, they had a whole different approach to it from what I had come to expect (especially of those from previous generations, such as my own).

This gives me hope that, through the emerging generations of leaders, the approach of the Church to the subject of harm, abuse and injustice may just stand the chance of turning the tide and strengthening the legacy for those that follow. We still have so far to go. Change is beginning to happen and there are these green shoots of hope across the Church. But for those who are still experiencing injustice, oppression, prejudice, especially victims and survivors of abuse from within the Church, this change is nowhere near quick enough, as we will explore a little later.

Making a difference and reaching a goal

So what exactly is needed from leaders in this task of making change happen in order to make a difference to the lives of others? Well part of it is about recognizing the purpose for pursuing change in the first place. As this opening sentence indicates, I am suggesting that change should lead to something tangible that makes a difference. We've heard on countless occasions that the job of the leader is to be clear about where we are going and how we are going to get there. Instilling confidence in those around us that we are worth following to that place in that manner. But do we always find agreement about the route we are proposing to get somewhere, or the methods we are employing along the way? I suspect not.

When my children were very young, my wife had the unfortunate experience of having to think swiftly on her feet to rescue our son (who was probably about three at the time – certainly pre-school) from a traumatic sequence of events. Starting from the end (which turned out to be OK) and working backwards, the story involves my son being brought into the house by his older sister (who was only three years older than he was) screaming and covered in blood. He had collided with the brick wall at the bottom of our slightly sloping back garden. As my wife began to question our daughter about what had happened, it became clear that this was the result of a rather poorly executed plan.

It turns out that she had catapulted her little brother into the air from a small child's seesaw, following which he had rolled down the slope before being stopped by the brick wall. But what exactly had they been doing, my wife asked, to which came the reply, 'we had this idea to kidnap the puppies from the garden next door'. It was obvious that our daughter had a clear goal in mind (albeit ill-conceived), but the execution of the plan had not been so great. Of course, our three-year-old son was never going to be successfully catapulted over the five-foot-high fence in 'Cirque du Soleil' fashion, land on his feet and be able to retrieve the dogs from under the nose of our neighbour. Instead, it all ended in tears and a trip to the local A&E to get our son's forehead glued back together. This event has affectionately become known in the family ever since as 'the failed dog heist'. Possibly a bad example, but the point is that we need both the goal and some idea that the plan we have in mind will help us get there.

Often as leaders, we may be in the position where we have inspired our followers sufficiently about the destination, but we have yet to convince them about the route or the method. I think this is OK and probably far more representative of where many of us find ourselves – especially when we are navigating new territory or there is a degree of uncertainty about exploring old problems in new ways.

Let's rewind a little and think how that might apply to this notion of church-based or clergy abuse for a moment. Where people have experienced the extreme injustice of being abused by a church leader, we need to think very carefully about how we are going to assist them and how the systems we may employ will be used sensitively. All too often in such scenarios, that ugly sense of self-protectionism or institutional protectionism gets in the way and derails any good effort or intentions. Sadly, we also see those who may have started out with good intentions becoming 'assimilated into the rotten structure' as it was put by a friend and clergy-abuse survivor. This is an important point to make here.

Making change happen and making a difference is hard work – don't let anyone fool you to think otherwise. It is also the case that, sometimes, the end goal may not always seem palatable to everyone, and the process of getting there may contain some pain – but at least knowing that the result is the right thing to pursue will help us. In discussing the challenges of navigating different cultural landscapes, Ken Wytsma puts it like this: 'Diagnosis is a bittersweet form of good news. It can be disappointing, shocking, even devastating; but it's a relief to finally know the truth.'[5]

Where a culture has yet to grasp and embed the need for root and branch change, the going will be tough and there will probably be casualties along the way. The pursuit of truth and justice will bring us to some of the most challenging points in our careers as we navigate the clash of perspectives and motivations. If we want to make a difference, we have to be prepared to go the distance! Reflecting on the words of Barack Obama at the beginning of this chapter, it is simply a case of rolling-up our sleeves and getting on with it. Waiting around for the change to happen will not make it happen. We have to be the change we want to see!

Reflections

1 Why not take some time to ask God to break your heart with what is breaking his?
2 Where might injustice be taking root, needing you to act now to be the change?
3 Where do you need to be the change that you want to see?

When abuse is discovered it is important that it is fully brought into the light so that justice can be served and those that have been affected can receive the help they need. We will not cover-up or collude but be open, transparent, and truly repentant about what has happened.

SAFER PLACES PLEDGE, THIRTYONE:EIGHT[1]

14

Concealing nothing

JUSTIN HUMPHREYS

Stories that should never be repeated

My parents were avid family researchers. What I mean is that they enjoyed spending hours and days researching their family history. On occasions, they would book an overnight hotel and travel to London to the National Archives and spend hours poring over the minutiae of detail that might lead them to join the dots and establish another link connecting the existing family tree to a new branch. One day, when I was probably still only in my late teens, I remember having a conversation with my parents about the discoveries they made and the stories they had uncovered about various ancestors.

There were all sorts of stories which could be celebrated. 'Thomas the tailor' was the first in a long line of ancestors in the 1700s who had been given the 'Freedom of the City of Exeter', through the generations as far as 'Stephen the cordwainer' in 1818, all for their contribution to industry in the city and wider area. But there were also the sorts of 'stories that should never be repeated' like the ancestor who had taken his own life by drinking sulphuric acid – a story which, when rarely told, always seemed to be followed by a macabre analysis of just how long and painful this must have been. But worse still was the story of the discovery that we had a highwayman in our lineage. This, I was told, was a story that my grandma had never allowed the family to speak of. The shame that she and those that went before her felt was so great that this was an episode in our family history that was better forgotten – never to be exposed by discussion.

I tell this tale slightly 'tongue in cheek' to make a point, but the reality is that concealing the truth is sadly a choice that leaders make every day in an attempt to avoid discrimination, exploitation, abuse and misconduct being scrutinized. These leaders will go to great lengths to maintain the dark secrets that they hold or to keep their skeletons well and truly in the closet.

> Dark secrets . . . are facts a person or organization knows and conceals because if they are revealed, they could damage the image or reputation of that person or organization. Allegations of abuse for example, are a common type of dark secret."[2]

At the outset of this chapter, it is important to say that a continued refusal to acknowledge and deal with hurt and abuse caused by individuals in our organizations (including those caused by ourselves) serves only to do further damage and re-abuse victims.

Lifting the lid

In a previous chapter I made reference to the work that my organization undertakes in completing 'Lessons Learned Reviews'. These are intensive and detailed assignments that are designed to 'lift the lid' on harmful events that have happened. The overall purpose of this is to identify what lessons can be learned so that such harm can be prevented in the future. We often use this phrase about lifting the lid in relation to such reviews as we are opening things up to scrutiny and shining a light into what has taken place – usually for the first time – and believe me, some places we have had to shine that light are incredibly dark! In many ways, this phrase refers to the point that we are focusing on within this chapter.

To conceal something means that active steps are taken to prevent something from being found or discovered. It is more than just omitting to mention details when asked (although this can also destroy trust and damage relationships). It is taking a decision to make sure that something remains hidden – sealing the lid down if you like. The origin of this word 'conceal' that we use today is Latin and derives from two words: *Con* (meaning completely) and *Celare* (meaning hidden). Following these Latin origins, the opposite of conceal could therefore be transparent, as follows: *Trans* (meaning through) and *Parere* (meaning appear).

In many ways, there would be no need for the many statutory inquiries that are held if organizations and their leaders took a more honest and transparent approach to events that have taken place. Such events span the interests of charity, corporate business, politics, entertainment, sport, religion and public service to name a few. Astonishingly, at the time of writing, there have been twenty-eight such inquiries (of which eleven are still active) launched in the UK by the government and the devolved administrations since the current framework was established by the Inquiries Act in 2005, at a cost to the public purse of £168m and rising.[3]

In case any should wonder the degree to which organizations and individuals of interest within the Christian world are a part of this, one only needs to look at the number of investigatory strands within the Independent Inquiry into Child Sexual Abuse that concern the wider Church to be clear. I suspect that the desire to protect reputations, finances and even God's name, if some were to be believed, is behind this reluctance towards learning lessons and facilitating justice. But what might be behind this often-used excuse or façade?

Time and time again, we are confronted with the fact that power and the human thirst for it is the culprit that lurks behind the most damaging of decisions. Those who believe they don't have it, want it. Those who already have (and wield) it, want more of it. In relative terms, we rarely hear of those that have power who genuinely and actively want to give it away for the benefit of others. No wonder that it often feels as though the lid needs to be prised-off, rather than simply lifted in order to establish the truth!

Defended vulnerability

As just leaders, we have a responsibility to operate with honesty and integrity. The humility that is required to stand in front of those that respect us and look to us for direction and to admit that we got it wrong is counter-intuitive. In our brokenness, our default position is so often to hold out and see if the storm will pass, or keep our heads down and hope that nobody will notice. Our own fragility, weakness and defended vulnerability cause us to be the very opposite of what (or who) we are called to be as leaders. This is helpfully illustrated by Padfield as he considers the hopeful influence we struggle to bring to our world:

Anyone who has held a position of significant leadership will tell you the myriad ways our human soul is fractured constantly manifests as counterweights to the way of angels. We are shot through with holes, and our need for significance, security and identity comes through even more forcefully, and with selfish twists and connotations, when we have increasingly powerful ways of meeting those needs.[4]

Please don't misunderstand me when I make reference to the negative aspects of our vulnerability. It is not that I am suggesting there is necessarily anything wrong with that vulnerability. However, when we hide it and refuse to deal with the root causes of that vulnerability (that is we refuse to engage in self-reflection and open ourselves up to the searching of the Holy Spirit) we create blind spots and footholds for the enemy to exploit to the detriment of those around us. These footholds are often what will ultimately trip us up and cause further damage to us and to others. Yet it is in this refusal to fully acknowledge the truth about ourselves and others where we find the desire to conceal truth rather than face it. In other words, we are being defensive, or even developing unhealthy strategies for control, rather than 'leading out of who we are' as described by Walker.

> These are not the markers of the just leader that we need to see today. So, the question is – are you prepared to be that leader that pursues justice with humility (like the words of the prophet Micah challenge us to be) and might be prepared to own both your own mistakes and maybe even those of others, which might have been inherited from those who went before you? This is very much faith and courage in action, but very much what is required.[5]

Lust, abuse and betrayal

Do you remember the story of King David and Bathsheba? There are so many lessons for us in this, one of the most famous stories in the Bible. Essentially, what we find is an account of how David (God's chosen king) attempted to conceal his moral fall by committing a criminal act rather than face the consequences of his lustful actions.

First, we read that David essentially took what we might refer to as 'the second look':

> One evening David got up from his bed and walked around on the roof of the palace. From the roof he saw a woman washing. The woman was very beautiful, and David sent someone to find out about her. The man said, 'She is Bathsheba, the daughter of Eliam and the wife of Uriah the Hittite.'
> (2 Samuel 11.2–3)

At first sight, David saw Bathsheba and thought she was beautiful. OK, no problem there as such. The difficulty is, he then made efforts to find out about her – he took a second look. The seed of lustful corruption was then planted in his mind. He had the intention to take sexual advantage of her and he did.

There are a number of concerns about this, of course. First, and perhaps most obviously, David had sexual relations with a woman who was not his wife. Indeed, he knew that she was also the wife of another man. Second, and perhaps more subtly or less explored, is that this was further compounded by the fact that he was king – a man of great power, influence and renown. This was a huge abuse of power and position.

Apart from the fact that David is described earlier in the book of 1 Samuel as 'glowing with health and . . . a fine appearance and handsome features' (1 Samuel 16.12), we have to assume that his position must have played a huge part in the interaction between them. We don't read anything of Bathsheba's perspective within this short account but, regardless, when holding such a position of power and influence, a greater level of awareness is required and a greater degree of responsibility expected. One might be forgiven for asking: how could she have refused his advances?

Then David makes a bad situation even worse. The story tells us that Bathsheba's husband Uriah was a good, loyal man. He fought for David against his enemies and refused to return to his home in between battles but stayed with his fellow soldiers instead. Once David had discovered that his illicit affair was to produce a child, he schemed to remove the possibility of his exposure by ensuring the death of Uriah on the frontline of battle:

> In the morning David wrote a letter to Joab and sent it with Uriah. In it he wrote, 'Put Uriah out in front where the fighting is fiercest. Then withdraw from him so he will be struck down and die.' So while Joab had the city under siege, he put Uriah at a place where he knew the strongest defenders were. When the men of the city came out and fought against Joab, some of the men in David's army fell; moreover, Uriah the Hittite died.
> (2 Samuel 11.14–17)

In essence, David has become the orchestrator of the ugliest concealment. We don't read in the story that David explains to anybody what he had done with Bathsheba. He didn't appear to make himself accountable to anyone. All we read is that he made great efforts to stop the truth from being brought into the light and to prevent the chance of his own discovery as a corrupted leader who took another man's wife.

A different path

Let's stay with this story for a while longer to think about what might have happened if he had confessed to his offence with Bathsheba. It would be good to think that, in other circumstances, with the benefit of hindsight, humility and a greater degree of self-control, David would not have slept with Bathsheba in the first place. This would have avoided the initial abuse of power that took place and not caused the damage (spiritually, relationally and otherwise) to Bathsheba. You see, considering the impact on Bathsheba in this scenario first, is exactly what we would describe as putting victims and survivors first (see Chapters 6 and 7). She was his victim. She succumbed to his power and position in a way that she should never have had to. Her agency to refuse would without question have been minimized by who David was.

Even if avoiding giving in to his temptations wasn't possible, he could certainly (one would hope) have avoided the need to murder her husband (another victim of his actions). So many times, when active efforts are made to conceal the truth, we see additional and unnecessary collateral damage caused to others. A further refusal to face the facts and deal with the hurts and offences that people have caused and committed when confronted by their victims just brings further damage.

There was an opportunity for David to choose a different path, to show a degree of authenticity in his leadership. In his weakness and brokenness, he chose to sin and then chose to sin further in his attempt to conceal what he had done. He could have chosen to confess and make himself accountable, even if he had already committed one abuse of power. This may have cost him dearly. He may never again have been regarded as the leader he once was. He may even have lost his position entirely – we will never know. But in choosing a different way, he may have been able at least to become an example of how to repent and begin making reparations with those he had sinned against.

In the end, one thing that is certain is that the wages of his sin were made so much greater by not addressing the offence when he had the chance. The damage caused by the initial offence brought its own consequences, but the damage by his attempts to conceal that offence made it yet worse as suggested by this anonymous author when writing of the destructive use of non-disclosure agreements in Christian organizations:

> . . . if a reputational damage crisis is not handled correctly early on, it becomes harder to manage as it is escalated up the chain of command. Each progression requires more courageous leadership to address the problem, while the risk of damaging fallout increases.[6]

Within the context of the Church, this damage is further described in the powerful chapter by Adrian Hilton within *Letters to a broken church* where he utilizes the words of Dietrich Bonhoeffer as a backdrop and reflects on the concealing of abuses by clergy within the Church of England:

> Cheap grace offends against the gospel, but nowhere near as much as a cheap episcopal cover-up. Both represent an abuse of ecclesial power, but the latter is arguably greater because the knowledge of

evil is concealed by deceit or denied altogether, and that breaches faith and trust.[7]

Agents of secrecy – the use of non-disclosure agreements

So far in this chapter, we have explored the deliberate actions of those who would seek to maintain secrecy surrounding unjust, adverse or harmful events that have occurred. We must remember that actions to conceal facts and events do not exist in a vacuum. There are often others who will be swept along and damaged by the self-serving and self-protecting actions of these agents of secrecy.

The remainder of this chapter will focus on one increasingly common and insidious practice employed by those seeking to maintain silence – the use of non-disclosure agreements (NDAs). While the origins of such measures may have been entirely legitimate (for example to protect commercially sensitive information from being shared), the use of such tools to buy the silence of whistle-blowers and those who have been treated unjustly has brought a new and deeply problematic practice into being.

In the many years that I have worked within safeguarding, I have maintained the view that the use of NDAs may well be appropriate as a way of preventing the unlawful or problematic disclosure of corporate proprietary information, but they should never be used in safeguarding cases as a means of removing a worker or leader following a disclosure or allegation of abuse or misconduct. NDAs were never designed for this context and are hugely damaging to all concerned when they are used in this way: 'By enforcing confidentiality and introducing a sense of legal intimidation, NDAs prevent organisational learning, undermine transparency and accountability and they discourage the restoration of relationships.' (Anon.)

In this observation, the writer makes the point that, as a tool, NDAs risk creating the very thing that opposes the practice of openness and transparency. It is the ultimate tool of concealment. It may be fair to say that in some circumstances an NDA may be in force and may have been entered into for an entirely different (and appropriate) reason rather than to cover-up abuse or harassment, let's say. However, such revelations should not fall within the terms of the NDA and therefore render the signatories complicit in such a cover-up, as suggested by Carter:

> At the organizational level, churches and ministries can also narrow the scope of confidentiality agreements. They can more clearly outline what areas truly warrant discretion (such as counseling or member giving) and where publicly notifying the larger body of Christ would be warranted (such as attempts to cover up abuse).[8]

Preventing disclosure (or 'gagging') in circumstances where abuse has been alleged or even proven is of itself a re-abuse of the victims and/or whistle-blowers. We only need to do a quick visit to our online search engine to see that this has been the case in settings across the spectrum, including churches, charities, corporates and others. The damage done to those who have been subjected to the inappropriate use of NDAs is clear to see and indefensible. However, there is another matter of major concern . . .

Discovery and justice

Some years ago, I had been retained as a safeguarding consultant to conduct and review a number of risk assessments and to ensure the organization was discharging its duties in the absence of a permanent post-holder. While engaged in this work, I became aware of a case involving the ex-headteacher of a large secondary school. It was clear that multiple allegations of inappropriate behaviour and misconduct had been made and that significant concern had been expressed over a prolonged period about his suitability to hold such a role working with young people. The statutory authorities had extensive involvement in this and took the decision that in order to avoid potential litigation, they would resolve the matter through enforcing an NDA within a severance package and let him go.

This may on the surface seem harmless, but what transpired was that the organization I was working for later became responsible for the activities this ex-headteacher was found to be involved with as a volunteer, in this case, leading a children's choir. The difficulty that had been caused by this inappropriate use of an NDA was that neither he nor the previous employer were permitted to discuss the past events and ultimately only a far from accurate reference could be supplied regarding his suitability:

> What happens often is that someone will leave an institution over some sort of misconduct and will quietly sign some severance agreement, then the institution can't really give any sort of detailed reference to the next institution that hires that person.[9]

This sort of situation has become all-too familiar in many settings, including churches and Christian charities, and it is highly dangerous. It undermines the creation of safer places, eliminates the discovery of truth and destroys the effective pursuit of justice for those affected.

Reflections

1 Where might you need to admit that you have got something wrong and bring it out into the open?
2 How can you encourage a culture of openness and transparency in your organization?
3 How can you ensure that in your sphere of influence the quest for justice is not thwarted by a misplaced desire to protect the reputation of the organization?

Nothing in all creation is hidden from God's sight. Everything is uncovered and laid bare before the eyes of him to whom we must give account.

(HEBREWS 4.13)

15

Holding ourselves accountable

JUSTIN HUMPHREYS

It starts with our vulnerability

If we are honest, how many of us are prepared to be answerable for our deepest failures? How many of us go out of our way and make ourselves vulnerable with another person to the point that we offer an account of those things that we would rather keep hidden? There is no question that practising accountability is a discipline – one that hopefully gets a little easier the more we do it. The difficulty is that, for many, the thought of being accountable to another person is so challenging that they spend inordinate amounts of time working out how to get around it.

Why is that? I suspect that much of it has its roots in a fear of failure, a dislike of challenge or criticism and the risk of seeing the darkest parts of ourselves brought into the light. Perhaps that's natural, so it becomes even more important to accept that this is a new way that will take effort. It starts with our own preparedness to be vulnerable and to do away with the shame, fear and control that holds us. In her bestselling book *Daring Greatly* Brené Brown uncovers from her own extensive research the reason why we find this one of the most difficult tasks:

> Our rejection of vulnerability often stems from our associating it with dark emotions like fear, shame, grief, sadness, and disappointment – emotions that we don't want to discuss, even when they profoundly affect the way we live, love, work and even lead.[1]

I must be clear right at the start of this chapter that accountability is only any good for us (and those around us) if we practise it freely and as a result of our own choice. Enforced accountability (and thereby vulnerability), as much as enforced silence that comes from cover-up and concealing truth, is hugely counter-productive and damaging. In fact, what we know from years of working with individuals and organizations that have experienced institutional and spiritual abuse is that this is one of the key hallmarks in a coercive and controlling leadership model.

Individualism vs togetherness

As I write this in 2020, I am aware of just how much attention is still given to individual performance and success. As we discussed in the last chapter, the tendency to celebrate that success still often seems to manifest itself in the adulation of the individual. Relatively little attention seems to be given to the successes of teams to the extent that we have a clear sense that everybody brought something to the party.

In my book, *Escaping the Maze* I spent some time challenging the risk of putting our leaders on pedestals, of idolizing them.[2] This is a dangerous preoccupation that puts leaders in a place of extreme risk and vulnerability and blinds us to the reality of their confidence and competence. It also increases the risk of nurturing unhealthy characteristics within our organizational culture. The point I am making here is that we must make great efforts to avoid this individualism in favour of togetherness. Togetherness with others who are able to bring what we do not have; to be honest and loving towards us in challenge to our egos and to keep our feet on the ground.

Togetherness should not be used to better our own chances and personal successes as we so often see. It is about seeing the long journey ahead and recognizing that we are far better to be with others on that journey than racing ahead alone. As someone said: it is a marathon, not a sprint. There are definitely occasions when is it not wise to race to be first, but plan to be second (or even last if this enables us to stay the course to the end with our confidence and integrity intact).

Thirtyone:eight is a rare organization. Not only is it pioneering in its safeguarding work with faith communities, it is unusual in the way that it is structured. When our last CEO moved on, the charity faced some difficult decisions. Should it carry on as it had before, or should it choose a different way? During the period of interregnum, while we had no CEO, the board came to recognize that something quite remarkable had started to take shape.

My colleague Steve and I had agreed to both step up together and lead the organization while decisions were made about the best way forward in recruiting a new CEO. What we all discovered was that this temporary, dual-executive model of leadership that we'd fallen into actually worked! Long story short, we proposed to the board that we continue with this model rather than seeking to appoint a single CEO in the traditional way.

Five years on, we continue with this arrangement of dual leadership. So what is it that makes this such a positive arrangement? Essentially, we have a model that shares responsibility and fosters accountability. We are safe to have conversations together that challenge each other and the plans we are making. We have enough openness and honesty in the relationship to invite constructive criticism about the things we have done or said. We know that we can confidently use each other as a sounding board based on the fact that we both bring something different and complementary to the task of leading a multi-million-pound organization. This is togetherness!

Depth of field

In recent times, I have returned to an old hobby. I have rekindled my love of photography and enjoy finding the next interesting image – whether it's portraits, architecture, landscapes, street scenes . . . I will try not to bore you too much with the geeky details, but there is a valuable analogy that we can use from this as we develop an understanding that leading justly requires us to be clear about who we are, what we are called to do and the context in which we are operating. In photographic terms, we need to increase the depth of field in order to see this clearly.

One option that photographers are always faced with is whether to stop the aperture of our lens right down or open it right up. This is the process of managing the amount of light that comes through the lens to hit the sensor (or film in the good old days) and create the image. It also affects the depth of field, or how much of the image is in focus. Let me explain this a little. If I were taking a portrait against a busy urban background, I might want to open the lens aperture up to its maximum and let in as much light as I can. The effect of this will also be that it renders the background of the image blurry (what's known as bokeh), thereby reducing the depth of field and surrounding detail and encouraging the eye to see the main subject in isolation. For many photographers, it's all about the bokeh!

As an alternative, we might want to stop the aperture right down, which in many ways has the opposite effect – it increases the depth field, creates more even lighting and brings both the main subject and the surrounding detail into focus so that we can see the relationship between foreground and background. The photographer John Waire illustrated this point beautifully in a quote often attributed to him: 'In photography and in life, always look for the light. If you don't see it, bring it.'

When thinking about leadership, it is important that we resist the urge to focus solely on ourselves and instead make efforts to bring light and make ourselves accountable to the wider context in which we are operating. Leadership is not just about success with this metric or that metric, or even necessarily the overall growth of our organization. Fundamentally, it is about people. What have we done to encourage people around us? Have we been attentive to the needs of those within our sphere of influence who are disadvantaged, oppressed or simply lacking what we have? This is about putting our learning, power, influence, resources and gifts to work for the benefit of others and being prepared to be accountable for our actions in doing so.

Sadly, there are too many examples of leaders who are driven by the performance culture over authenticity. The saddest thing about this is that those leaders have seriously missed the most powerful tool they possess. It is as if they have blurred out the surroundings. They have failed to see the low-hanging fruit that was right in front of them. As leaders, our striving for authenticity will ultimately bring out the best in us and the best in those around us. Bringing those two ingredients together is a winning combination, in whatever context or setting we find ourselves; whether business, volunteering, hobbies, family life or marriage. What's often missing is the preparedness to hold ourselves accountable to others. This is the means by which we stay on track with our pursuit of authenticity.

Being deliberate about seeking out another person and being undefended in asking the searching questions is so important. How am I doing with this? What can I do better? Did you feel empowered in that situation? Did I value your contribution sufficiently? Was it about me or was it about us? Tell me where I went wrong! This in turn enables us to see ourselves more accurately within our context and understand better how we might assist others more effectively in their own pursuits, challenges and struggles.

A culture of honour

The trouble is that it is often hard to ask such searching questions about ourselves. Inviting criticism is not something we are typically good at. To have anybody confirm our own worst suspicions about ourselves, or point out that we may not be as good as we think we are, speaks deeply to our psyche. As a result, we guard our hearts and minds and put up barriers to our own learning. But here's the revelation: if we are truly doing whatever we do for God (rather than ourselves), then he alone is the assessor of our success. The good news is that God's measures of success are not the same as the world's. So even in our darkest or most challenging moments, we can hold on to the many promises and truths about ourselves, just as the Psalmist did: 'I praise you because I am fearfully and wonderfully made; your works are wonderful, I know that full well' (Psalm 139.14).

Why is it that we feel so exposed and vulnerable by becoming more of an open book to people around us? At the heart of the matter, we find that fear, shame and guilt are hard at work. Each of these prevents a true perspective of who we are and limits our appetite for accountability. We will look at the relationship between these three elements a little later on. For now, one of the most important truths for us to understand is that, if we truly honour each other, the path to both individual and collective improvement is more easily found. Creating a culture of honour where we put others before ourselves, deeply value the other, speak the best of each other and treat each other with true respect, facilitates a much better environment for accountability and authenticity, regardless of our own failures:

Honour looks past the imperfections and flaws that mar our appearances, our reputations, and looks right into the soul, seeing the treasure hidden in the darkness, the thing of beauty and value that will outlive the ugliness and disgrace.[3]

There are so many reasons to put what might seem a disproportionate effort into the development of healthier cultures in our organizations. Culture is the soil in which we hope our plans and purposes will flourish. No amount of good training, policies and workplace practices will achieve all that they are intended to if the culture in which they are planted is unhealthy or untended. We can either spend time cultivating fertile soil or we can neglect it and find that our best-laid plans and intentions fail to take root and flourish (see Figure 5).

A culture of deference

Within the institutional Church in the UK (and similarly worldwide), there remains a belief system and practice that does more to poison the fertile soil than will probably ever be fully understood. One of the most powerful sources of a toxic culture is the insistence on the archaic practice of deference. This may on the surface seem similar to that of honour, but in actual fact it could not be further from it. Honour is primarily given freely from one person to another, regardless of whether the recipient believes it is deserved. Deference is demanded, expected and spoken over

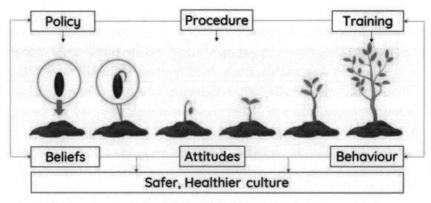

Figure 5 Planting in fertile ground

others in a manner that undermines, diminishes and devalues another person's sense of self.

Deference not only damages those that are held underneath its heavy weight, but it removes any notion of accountability and places the leader demanding it beyond the reasonable reach of anyone who might bring challenge or scrutiny. This was found to be a key element of the difficulties that had been exposed in the practices of the Church of England over countless decades, where hundreds (or likely thousands) were abused without any chance of proper justice or reparation:

> Power was vested chiefly in the clergy, without accountability to external or independent agencies or individuals. A culture of clericalism existed in which the moral authority of clergy was widely perceived as beyond reproach. They benefited from deferential treatment so that their conduct was not questioned, enabling some to abuse children and vulnerable adults.[4]

The 'loyalty card'

Similar to the effects of deference is the requirement for loyalty or obedience. Disguising secrecy and concealment as loyalty to the mission (or even to the leader him or herself) is a standard tactic of those leaders who seek to manipulate and control. The call to excessive commitment, time, obedience and other such areas are all often reinterpreted as loyalty by leaders who have no desire to see anything other than their own plans and ideas take shape within an organization. In the seminal text *The Subtle Power of Spiritual Abuse* Johnson and Van Vonderen expertly identify the subtlety of the abusive leader.[5] Much of this is in relation to the use of language and the implied messages that maintain their followers under a controlling regime.

In other words, all these unrealistic and unreasonable expectations are disguised as loyalty and loyalty equals a place in the inner circle with all the privileges and entitlements that this affords. When leaders operate this way, I call it playing the 'loyalty card'. Just like the card you keep for your favourite shop or store. The more it gets used, the more points you earn to draw down benefits. It's a trap and a mechanism for buying cooperation that becomes increasingly difficult to withdraw from.

Loyalty is a powerful thing. It causes us to lose perspective. Just like the shallow depth of field created with the camera lens, it has the ability to blur the edges and prevent us from seeing the landscape around the subject. For the leader who lacks accountability and authenticity, this is a key tool. This ever-present demand for loyalty is identified as a common feature in many of the modern day scandals that have engulfed the Christian leadership world in recent times. Reflecting on their research into the revelations from Willow Creek Church in Chicago, Scot McKnight and Laura Barringer refer to it as 'toxic loyalty' with deep roots: 'The seeds for loyalty were planted early in the history of Willow Creek and quickly became a deeply rooted feature of its culture. One can assume that everyone in any kind of leadership position was deeply loyal.'[6]

Any leader who truly seeks authenticity and understands accountability will never behave in this way. When the 'loyalty card' gets used by a leader it only serves to toxify the culture and undermine justice – in any context.

Developing your nose

My wife and I live in a large town on the Jurassic Coast (a world heritage site) in the south-west of England. When the busyness of life temporarily subsides, we like to take time to enjoy the beauty of our surroundings and the interesting things that go on within them. One of the local treasures we have enjoyed is a small, family-run vineyard that has been producing award-winning wines for some years – good enough even to rival some of the best we're told. We would not describe ourselves as connoisseurs by any stretch, but we do enjoy a glass or two. One year, one of our adult children bought us a 'wine tasting experience' at this local vineyard. It was fascinating. We walked through the vineyards learning about the soil, the vines, the different varieties of grape and the growing and harvesting process. We were even invited to return and help during the harvesting season. Best of all, we were then given the chance to taste the wines and learn about how they are produced.

As you probably know, there are a number of elements or stages to wine tasting; one is the palate (or taste) and another is the nose (or aroma).

With any wine, the expert can detect the various ingredients that may be present in a wine through its taste – even down to the type of soil the grape was grown in. They will also be able to develop a keen sense of the smell of the wine and whether it is sweet, sour, bitter or even salty. The sense of smell is highly tuned and is actually far more accurate than even our taste!

In my work with many groups and organizations over recent decades, I have come to be able to discern in a similar way some aspects of the culture that exists within them. On occasions, the tell-tale signs of unhealthy systems and cultural characteristics show themselves quite early. In others, they are more hidden and less easy to detect at first.

What is common in most of these scenarios is that the people within the system, or subject to the culture, are usually unaware until some crisis or incident strikes and they are forced to re-position themselves and gain new perspective and insight. This is a difficult process. It is this kind of discernment (or nose) that as leaders we need to develop. What can we see within our organizations (and sometimes within our own attitudes and behaviours) that might hinder the flourishing of others? Writing of the systemic damage done to organizations (and specifically churches) by a narcissistic leader, Chuck DeGroat says this:

> You can't see it, but it lurks among and between the relational spaces, in anxious bodies, and in flawed structures. It shows up in our ability to be personally and organisationally honest, to recognise the strengths and weaknesses of a church system, a denomination, or a network of churches. It shows up in our unwillingness to take intentional steps toward systemic healing.[7]

How can we pick up the subtle aromas of attitudes, beliefs and behaviours that threaten to cause problems for those we lead, before they totally infiltrate and infect the system and culture we are responsible for? You guessed it – one of the key ingredients we must look for is whether appropriate accountability mechanisms are in place at all levels – above us, below us and all around us. Holding ourselves accountable to each other provides us with an ongoing litmus test or temperature check and we should be careful not to ignore the results.

Reflections

1 How are you holding yourself accountable and what might you need to do to increase the accountability you have?
2 Where are you picking up the subtle aromas of attitudes, beliefs and behaviours that threaten to infiltrate your organization? How can appropriate accountability help you deal with this?
3 How are you modelling vulnerability to those you lead and others around you?

Part 3
JUST WORLD

Introduction to Part 3

Our vision and dream is of a generation of world-changers, a movement of *just leaders* who bear the hallmarks of coming close to injustice, who walk with victims and survivors, who use power well, who have the courage to tackle the difficult stuff and who speak out with grace and truth.

We hope that part two gave you an insight to the leadership attributes we believe are needed right now and the characteristics, skills and attitudes that you may need to build in order to be a *just leader*.

Matthew Frost, who was for many years the CEO of Tearfund, offered some great advice for leadership development and learning. He said that however brilliant we were at developing leaders, if we take them out of their organizations and put them back in without addressing the systemic issues inherent in their organization, then our impact would always be limited. He was and is so right!

So, as leaders, how do we address the injustice in our own organizations and what does it look like to build organizations full of just leaders who do justice and fashion organizations after their own image?

It is to this subject that we now turn as we ask the questions – what do a *just church*, a *just charity* and a *just business* actually look like, and what impact can they have on building a *just society* in which we all become image bearers of a just God?

It's especially important for those of us who come to the Bible from positions of relative social, economic, and racial privilege to read its stories alongside people from marginalized communities, past and present, who are often more practiced at tracing that crimson thread of justice through its pages.

RACHEL HELD EVANS[1]

16

Just church

JUSTIN HUMPHREYS

Justice must prevail

Isn't this quote from Rachel Held Evans on the previous page the truth! We have spent many pages considering what *just leadership* is: how it manifests itself, how it affects others and how it can shape our leadership culture and actions. This point about how our leadership and life experiences in general affect others is so powerful. Fundamentally, the focus of the Church should always be about achieving God's plans and purposes in our world. We should do this in a way that is prepared to see his world through the eyes of others, learn from their experience as much as our own and approach his word with at least that dual perspective as suggested by Held Evans. God was and is all about being and doing justice – that's in part at least why he sent Jesus. God was and is all about forgiveness, because after all if forgiveness was not ours for the receiving, Jesus would have died in our place for nothing. God is without question the God of second chances, new starts and rebirth. Not only did Jesus' death represent the deepest expression of love and forgiveness, his birth represents the very nature of the justice-focus that God so needed to remind us of: 'The thief comes only to steal and kill and destroy; I have come that they may have life, and have it to the full' (John 10.10).

Love and justice to replace hatred and injustice. For us to experience life to its fullest, justice must prevail and this surely must be a message that is lived out by the Church, his people. But how many of us see these words in action through the Church today amid a world that is tearing itself apart through selfishness, greed, intolerance, inequality and oppression? It is as though we have only opened one eye to look around us and see what is going on in the world – to see too clearly would bring us too much pain perhaps. Maybe we have failed to kneel long enough for God to reveal the depths of his own pain and to sufficiently direct our footsteps to intervene as suggested by the great C. S. Lewis: 'Have we ever risen from our knees in haste for fear God's will should become too unmistakable if we prayed longer?'[2]

I have to confess that I am often brought to my knees (almost literally) with shame and disbelief at the way the Church of today often behaves and what it seems to represent for the many who need its message of hope the most. Rather than being that relentless advocate of justice, righteousness, love and peace, it shows itself to be self-serving, disinterested and ignorant of the needs it is surrounded by. Please don't misunderstand me; I am a man of deep faith and belief in God and my relationship with God, although not always as good as it should be, is enduring. But as I write, holding back my own tears, I look at what we have made his Church and I feel sick to the pit of my stomach. I see little true justice at work in the lives of ordinary people. I see institutions, I see celebrity, I see dishonesty, I see abuse and it often seems that any good that might be done risks being eclipsed by these representations of folly and falsehood and a desire to protect itself, identified by Barnes:

> The church is supposed to be a place where we can find God's grace in life. But like every other institution, it is often more worried about itself than concerned about the individuals within it . . . When your church hurts you, at that moment you are as disgraced as the Samaritan woman who was left alone to undertake a lonely search for living water in the desert of her own soul.[3]

How Jesus must be weeping.

Forward movement – let justice roll

This feels like a very strong and hopeless opening to a chapter so late in this book – I get it. But it is time for the Church to wake up and smell the coffee. That means that the change we have spoken about in earlier chapters has to start with you and me and our practice of *just leadership*. This is the essence of the message that I brought to the Justice Conference held in London, when asked about the role of the Church in advocating for justice today: 'The Church cannot expect to have any credibility in the justice arena if it is incapable of addressing its own blind spots and dealing with the mess in its own back yard.'[4]

I know that when we face what appear to be unsurmountable challenges, one reaction can be to hide away and wallow in a sense of self-pity and despair, but this amounts to little more than self-inflicted paralysis. I refuse to do this. What we need to see is movement – forward movement that is not deterred by the naysayers and obstructors. Maybe the words of Amos can encourage us in this:

I hate, I despise your religious festivals; your assemblies are a stench to me. Even though you bring me burnt offerings and grain offerings, I will not accept them. Though you bring choice fellowship offerings, I will have no regard for them. Away with the noise of your songs! I will not listen to the music of your harps. **But let justice roll on like a river, righteousness like a never-failing stream!**
(Amos 5.21–24)

In that same conference in London in 2020, in front of the hundreds gathered, I had the privilege of giving voice to the account of a survivor of abuse. It's a painful story, but illustrative of the experiences of so many. It carries many of the dreadful hallmarks of how survivors of clergy abuse are often treated and the effects of their experiences on them, but it manages to maintain a glimmer of hope. I have been given permission to share this person's story anonymously here.

Coming from an evangelical background, I have always been familiar with the concept of 'being a witness'. It meant witnessing to the gospel, sharing your faith in Jesus.

A few years ago, I found myself a witness of a different sort. Soon after my mentor and former vicar was arrested on charges of child sexual abuse, I remembered a few things he'd said which at the time had seemed a little odd, but which I hadn't considered important.

This began to weigh on my mind. That was the start of a 15-month process.

My vicar had been the first person I had told of my childhood abuse, and he followed this up by a series of sessions of 'pastoral counselling', in which he had asked me every detail of the abuse. Much of the information I had to give the police concerned what he had said and done in these counselling sessions. Remembering this was doubly traumatic: not only did it mean retelling for a police statement the original abuse; but in doing so I began to realize the extent of his betrayal of me and the harm he had done me. And this was a man to whom I owed much of my spiritual formation. It was devastating.

The months dragged on, with the police coming back to me now and then with further questions. The pressure was enormous. A few weeks before the trial I was told that I would not be required to appear in court, which was a big relief. However, I was advised that this might change so I couldn't really relax.

Then came the trial itself and the evidence of the victims. It was appalling. I had somehow assumed that, although my vicar faced 36 counts of child sexual abuse, the assaults had not been very serious. Maybe I was just trying to convince myself. Instead, it emerged that, especially during his time as chaplain at a children's home, he had behaved with a cruelty bordering on sadism. Moreover, he had told the children that the abuse was part of his ministry. How do you cope with the knowledge that your spiritual mentor has been capable of such a blasphemy?

The archdeacon made an appointment to visit me; I assumed he wanted to see how I was following the trial. I was worn out, grieving my loss of contact with my vicar's family, and still reeling from the impact of what I had learned about him. I told the archdeacon I was struggling and felt I needed a three-day retreat in which I could work through the spiritual issues. He refused, saying he'd had a complaint I wasn't doing enough work. Three weeks later I had a breakdown.

The prophet Amos has God saying:

'let justice roll down like waters,
    and righteousness like an ever-flowing stream.' (v. 24, NRSV).

If righteousness is going to continue to flow, the Church needs to do more than just make financial reparations – as right and necessary as those are. All senior personnel in the Church need to be much more aware of the enormous burden borne by those involved in abuse cases and be prepared to offer whatever support is needed. The survivors are the heroes.

When we do justice, we do God's work; justice is God's business and should be ours. Justice and redress have been a long time coming for too many of the Church's victims. Now, at last, may righteousness become a stream which flows through the Church – and keep on flowing.

I long for the day when the Church might again be seen as a pioneer in this fight for justice; where our actions match our words. Our credibility and the veracity of our words and actions depend on the Church living with integrity and being true to God's heart in this endeavour.

A determination to make a difference

These are without doubt difficult times we live in. We are currently finding our way through a global pandemic with local, national and international lockdowns and restrictions on trade and travel. The change and uncertainty that this brings can sometimes be overwhelming. Maybe we are just within a kind of liminal space at the moment. But let's see this as a time to reset rather than accept paralysis. What is this liminal space? It is the space in between what was and what is yet to be. You find yourself (literally, metaphorically or even mentally) in a place where you can't go back because what was no longer is. You can't move forward because what comes next is yet to become clear and available.

If we feel stuck in a liminal space, experiencing the paralysis of having left the past, but without confidence in stepping into the future, then maybe we have not seen this in-between period as a creative space of reflection and transition. So it may be like this with the role the Church has to play in the justice scene. Maybe we just need to hit the pause button, reset and enter a new chapter with a determination to make a difference to our world as we have been called to do. As Briner puts it:

> The test of the vitality of a religion is to be seen in its effect on culture. If a religion is really vital, meaningful, relevant and important, it will make a difference not only in the lives of individuals but also in society itself.[5]

Maybe this is the time (returning to the words of C. S. Lewis) to stay on our knees a little longer to hear God's voice calling us forward and re-igniting our passion for truth and justice in our world. If the Church is no longer the carrier of this hope – who else can be relied on?

Looking forward with hope

There comes a point when we may need to break from tradition, or the norms that have been, in order to see justice take shape in the lives of others around us. Doing what we always did will only get us what we always got. We need change if we are going to see a just Church rise above the dark shadow that engulfs it at times. We have a part to play in this alongside the rising generations – together we have a responsibility to set a new agenda and new way that learns from past mistakes and demonstrates real commitment to seeing good fruit. Padfield insightfully suggests:

> We have to change approach. We realise that the things we learned and embraced in our formation aren't necessarily the right things for those who come after us. The spotlight shines on the negative influences we embraced. And even when we got things right, sometimes life, culture and society changes and demands different qualities from those in the generations behind us.[6]

Whether we are focused on global poverty, climate change, equality and diversity, safer churches and communities, de-institutionalization of children, baby loss, law enforcement, or any other aspect of society in which we want to see justice, we must be inspired by the hope that things can (and must) change for good.

We have been here before!

Let's not kid ourselves into thinking that change will come overnight. We are going to have to work hard at it and bring our learning from the past to help shape our onward journey. In his work on resisting the 'quick fix' approach to leadership, Friedman reflects on the position of the Church, the arts and academia in previous times and the ability of society to push forward to reinvent itself, even when justice appeared far from view:

> Late fifteenth-century Europe, despite its glorious cathedrals, emerging artists, and developing network of universities, was a society living in the wake of the plagues, the breakdown of the feudal order, and the increasing inability of an often hypocritical and corrupt church's capacity to ring true . . .Over the next half-century, more radical change occurred in every field of human endeavour than had ever happened before.[7]

So you see – we have been here before. Whatever our context, whether feeling trapped by the paralysis of a pandemic lockdown or a crisis of confidence in government or religious institutions, change is possible. In fact, as Christians, we are called to 'be the change' and bringers of change – the change agents if you like. The purpose of being the 'town on a hill' was not that we should parade ourselves selfishly showing *our* glory while continuing to collude with the ways of the world or society, but that we should shed light on what surrounds us and exist as an example of what *should* be:

> You are the salt of the earth. But if the salt loses its saltiness, how can it be made salty again? It is no longer good for anything, except to be thrown out and trampled underfoot.

> You are the light of the world. A town built on a hill cannot be hidden. Neither do people light a lamp and put it under a bowl. Instead they put it on its stand, and it gives light to everyone in the house. In the same way, let your light shine before others, that they may see your good deeds and glorify your Father in heaven.
> (Matthew 5.13–15)

You and me as the body

The Independent Inquiry into Child Sexual Abuse in the UK has just concluded its investigation into safeguarding within the Anglican Church. Amid the flurry of media attention and the running commentary on social media platforms, there is a seldom-explored message. What typically happens when an organization or individual is publicly found wanting or, worse still, guilty of a great injustice, is a distancing from them by a multitude of critics. This is easy to do because when we see something that offends us, those who are justice-minded feel compelled to speak out – and that is right!

What we sometimes don't appreciate is that when Christians speak up against other Christians critically, some degree of respect is too often lost. When we criticize 'the Church' for its failings, we forget that we are part of the Church too. The way in which we speak out needs to appreciate that, to the onlooker, we might as well be a part of the problem – and maybe this should alter the way we communicate at these times. As Paula Gooder suggests in this pearl of wisdom, when one person offends, it is never just that one person offends (as bad as that is) – it has an impact on and relates to all of us:

> The actions of an individual are never just the actions of an individual. What one person does affects the whole . . . One of the reasons why Christianity struggles to find a natural home in the modern Western world is because Christianity is underpinned by an understanding of corporate identity, in which who you really are can only be understood together rather than apart.[8]

This is why the comment I made a moment ago has such poignancy. In a recent exchange on Twitter, a survivor made the following point:

> We need to stop making it 'their' fault so 'they' need to do something. We are the Church, so we're all responsible . . . If we're not abusers, we are witnesses, bystanders, colluders. And we're creators, rebuilders, advocates. We need to stop saying, 'they need to change' and ask 'how do I need to change?'

I can't agree more. We ARE the Church and if we want to see justice done and change demonstrated, it starts with us!

These are the beginnings of a just Church.

So what are the hallmarks of a just Church at the end of all this? Maybe they look something like this:

- a people that understand that God is all about justice and that this is not a pick and mix scenario for us to endorse what is comfortable and reject what is difficult;
- a people that understand the importance of nurturing relationships: both within and outside their number towards a more inclusive, equitable and fair society;
- a family that understands that it is a body – bringing different skills, gifts, abilities and experiences, and that when one part suffers, we all suffer;
- a community that understands that it has both a collective and individual responsibility to model justice and to take action where injustices are given space to breathe, where abrogation of responsibility is not an option;
- a community that learns from the mistakes of the past and is resolute in its commitment not to repeat them which would be to the detriment of those they are called to serve.

Reflections

1 How do you measure against the hallmarks of a just Church?
2 Where are the remaining examples of injustice within your Church or sphere of influence and what impact might they have on the credibility of your efforts to seek justice for others?
3 How might you be able to bring lessons from the past to positively influence your actions (or those of others) as a just leader?

Do nothing out of selfish ambition or vain conceit. Rather, in humility value others above yourselves, not looking to your own interests but each of you to the interests of the others.

(PHILIPPIANS 2.3–4)

17

Just charity

JUSTIN HUMPHREYS AND SIMON BARRINGTON

Charity-minded

What does it mean to be charity-minded in the context of *just leadership*? Do charity and justice even sit well together? What does a *just charity* look like and how should a just leader approach being charitable? Before we get to those questions, though, it's interesting to stop for a moment and think about what 'charity' or 'being charitable' means. If we're honest, the word has become synonymous with charitable organizations or simply charities – those that are registered with the respective government office as providing some form of public benefit. This is OK to a point as it provides us with some understanding of what this is all about, but does it go far enough? We will return to organizations as charities shortly. In the meantime, is there a risk that we overlook something deeper?

If you've ever researched this, you might have been comforted to find that the Bible has plenty to say about charity. The verse at the beginning of this chapter gives us a clear guide regarding the motivation for being charitable, or charity-minded. It is a selfless state of being that does the opposite of any activity that is self-serving or conceited.

In fact, it suggests to us that it is all about looking to the needs of others. What is perhaps most beautiful about this particular passage of Scripture is that it is set within a chapter that is all about imitating the humility of Jesus. Some of the words later in this passage may well be better-known to many, but it is good that we wait here for a moment and consider what this might be saying to us in the context of *just leadership*.

Imitating Christ's humility

Therefore if you have any encouragement from being
united with Christ, if any comfort from his love, if
any common sharing in the Spirit, if any tenderness
and compassion, then make my joy complete by
being like-minded, having the same love, being
one in spirit and of one mind. Do nothing out of
selfish ambition or vain conceit. Rather, in humility
value others above yourselves, not looking to your
own interests but each of you to the interests of the
others.

In your relationships with one another, have the same
mindset as Christ Jesus:

who, being in very nature God,
did not consider equality with God something to be
used to his own advantage;
rather, he made himself nothing
by taking the very nature of a servant,
being made in human likeness.
And being found in appearance as a man,
he humbled himself
by becoming obedient to death–
even death on a cross!
Therefore God exalted him to the highest place
and gave him the name that is above every name,
that at the name of Jesus every knee should bow,
in heaven and on earth and under the earth,
and every tongue acknowledge that Jesus Christ is Lord,
to the glory of God the Father.
(Philippians 2.1–11)

The grand plan

This passage in Philippians speaks of unity, relationship, sharing, love
and compassion. All these things go before, as a precursor to the plea that
we imitate or are like-minded with Christ Jesus in our acts of service and

charity to others. The key to all this is that Jesus as our model represents the blueprint for humility and servant leadership.

We cannot be just leaders if we are not servant leaders, authentic leaders or, dare we say, Christian leaders. There was nothing self-serving in Jesus' actions – ever! He was all about doing his Father's business, restoring relationships and drawing his creation back to himself to once again experience that complete peace and harmony that he originally intended – this was and has always been the grand plan. This is the backdrop against which we perhaps ought to look at what charity seems to be in our society today and how we might exercise *just leadership* as our part in this grand plan.

Is charity just a distraction?

There sometimes appears to be what might be described as 'spiritual snobbery' that exists in some corners of the Church, taking a view that is so purist as to dismiss anything that doesn't immediately appear within a relatively narrow sweep of the radar. On occasions, we might hear people say things like, 'that [insert your own activity or issue] isn't important to the true gospel message. It's just a distraction. Let's get on with the real mission and ministry of the Church'. In the context of a broken and searching world, these attitudes are troubling in today's society as they undermine the opportunities that we all have, every day, to be the 'hands and feet of Jesus' in some of the darkest and most challenging corners of our communities. John Stott suggests that our ability to do this is: 'The expenditure of energy (manual or mental or both) in the service of others, which brings fulfilment to the worker, benefit to the community, and glory to God.'[1] Sounds like charity doesn't it? So, let's ask ourselves the question: is all this charity stuff, all this 'good works' stuff just a distraction? Of course, we would argue not – this *is* the mission and ministry of the Church. It is the very essence of our relationship with God the Father and the outworking of what he has called us to. These things require us be in relationship with others, to visit the margins, to reach out to the oppressed and give of what we have (financially, emotionally, physically, spiritually and otherwise). We cannot meet him without this as Ken Wytsma argues:

'We don't stray away from good doctrine or truth by focusing on justice and compassion for those in the margins – rather, we find Jesus and truth *in* the margins.'[2]

So, returning to the question of charity and its relevance to *just leadership* – the two go hand-in-hand in Scripture. As Simon noted in Chapter 9, loosing chains and feeding the hungry are fundamental parts of our worship:

> Is not this the kind of fasting I have chosen: to loose the chains of injustice and untie the cords of the yoke, to set the oppressed free and break every yoke? Is it not to share your food with the hungry and to provide the poor wanderer with shelter – when you see the naked, to clothe them . . . ?
> (Isaiah 58.6–7)

As just leaders we must also be charity-minded. We must find ways to give of what we have to others. For many of us (ourselves included), this will manifest in our service as charity leaders and in furthering the charitable work we are privileged to lead. Knowing what God has called us to and why it is essential to playing our part in furthering his mission here on earth. As John Mark Comer puts it:

> Work is serving. Often when we talk about vocation and calling, it's a conversation about self-fulfilment. And that's not all bad, but it goes south really fast. We're followers of Jesus. We believe that fulfilment is found in giving our life *away*, not hanging on to it. Jesus was a servant. So are we. So, where does the world need people to serve?[3]

Faith-inspired and faith-driven

At some point in the early 1990s, I (Justin) was faced with being made redundant from the first career I had chosen. I worked in photography and loved it. I was devastated to find that the economic recession in the UK was bringing an end to a dream. While in the place of seeking God and searching that followed, I was given a book *Broken windows, broken lives* by

Adrian Plass.[4] I can't recall who gave it to me or even if they intended that I should return it (which I didn't by the way as I still have the copy on my bookshelf that Adrian later signed for me), but reading it was one of those catalyst moments. I heard God's voice loud and clear through the pages of the story about Dennis, the young, 'maladjusted boy' and David who was to find his new career working with Dennis and others.

The story I was reading had so many parallels with my own that it was almost as if I was reading a surreal interpretation of my own life. From that point onwards, I knew that God was calling me to a ministry with children and young people and specifically those who had been damaged and traumatized by their early experiences of life. Some would say that the rest is history. I certainly heard the call and it was the beginning of me giving something of what I had to others in great need. Thirty years later, leading a national Christian safeguarding charity, this is still my call.

You see, I believe that there is something really powerful in our ability as Christians to have an impact in the lives of others through a faith-inspired and faith-driven mission, worked out through a charitable organization. In my case, one that has a clear and unwavering commitment to justice and protection for the most vulnerable in our society.

The origins of charity in the UK

At the start of this chapter, we explored one of the many and most helpful passages of Scripture to help us understand what charity is all about from a biblical perspective (Philippians 2.3–4). We have also taken a brief look at what charitable activity might look like as a response to the wider call to justice through the Church and charitable activities.

A search for the origins of the word 'charity' that we use today shows that it derives from the Latin *carus* and *caritas* and was later translated into old French as *charite* and finally into old English as *charity*. This old English translation basically means 'Christian love of one's fellows'. So again we are brought full circle to this idea of charity and charitable activities being inextricably linked to the Christian faith.

Although Christians can be seen at the heart of charitable activities in the UK from as early as the sixth century (The King's School,

Canterbury), they began to gather significant momentum as a means of establishing justice in various forms from the fourteenth century onwards and were largely seen as synonymous with the Church, as noted by Sir Stephen Bubb:

> Charity and giving were core to the Christian faith and in the early centuries of development it is hard to see charity as a separate entity from the church itself. Indeed, the early British would not have seen a charity industry at all, just one aspect of church activity . . . In essence, up to the Reformation, we see charity as largely faith-based and faith-driven, and a set of endeavours whose role was essentially to provide the welfare services for the citizenry in place of the state.[5]

In his commentary on the development of the British charity, Bubb paints a picture of the Christian Church playing an unparalleled part in the overall development of modern British life, served by the existence of countless charities working for the good of others in a wide range of endeavours. This is justice at work and, although current society has many problems, deficiencies and complications, we would do well to consider the alternative situation had Christ's followers not sought to be active in their faith, again as described by Bubb:

> Without the third sector, we could now be living in an England that resembles the worst of William Blake's Dark Satanic mills. Imagine the fields, woodlands and glades of the country built over for railways, factories and stockpiles. Imagine children were still sent to do heavy work 12 hours a day, toiling along with their parents in vile conditions for pittance pay, flanked by beasts of burden being slowly worked to death. Worse, imagine they are toiling alongside a host of slaves trapped in a never-ending Industrial Revolution. Imagine there are no rights to gender equality, with dissent landing you in a privately-run, privately owned prison. Imagine a towering inferno, and the recovery led by the Royal Borough of Kensington & Chelsea. Perhaps extreme, but as we will see, both the campaigning and the service delivery functions of charity have been central to the development of integral cornerstones of modern British life.

Charities as catalysts for hope and change

Many of us continue in this strong tradition today, motivated by our Christian faith and playing our part in reaching out to those in greater need through the work of charities, whether through making donations, working or volunteering. In England and Wales alone, just short of 45,000 charities are registered with the Charity Commission as providing religious activities.[6] Of course, these would be inspired by a wide range of religions, but this is still a significant proportion of charities overall (currently estimated at 168,000).[7]

There is good news that, for many Christians, there is a deep motivation to be charitable towards others which generates a higher than average impact through actions such as financial giving. In their study of poverty activism among UK and US Christians, the Barna Group.[8] discovered that seventy-three per cent of Christians donate to charities, compared to sixty-three per cent of all others and that sixty-nine per cent of Christians had done so in the past year, compared to sixty-two per cent of the remaining population sampled.

This is all very encouraging, but as we said earlier, all this activity focused on justice through a range of charitable activities needs to draw us back to knowing our 'why', as Ken Costa puts it.[9] Without this understanding of why, we are only likely to achieve a small part of what is possible and be able to convince others that this motivation is sound, as Paula Gooder suggests : 'In my view, what we need to do is to get better at talking about why Christian faith motivates us to show the love of Christ in the world – the "why we do what we do" question.'[10]

And this brings us all the way back to what we looked at in Chapter 1. Understanding a just God and exploring how our love for him and desire to be in relationship with him can transform our lives, as well as those around us, is fundamental to this whole question of what *just leadership* is all about. So being charitable may only be a part of how we seek justice and act with justice, but it seems as though it is a really important part.

Whether we consider ourselves to be on the front line of activism through work with charitable organizations, or whether we are bringing our understanding of justice to bear on our everyday attitudes, behaviours and decisions, maybe this concept of charity can be a catalyst for hope and change.

Are all charities just?

It is clear that charities as organizations have existed in different forms for many centuries, but what is it that we can expect of them in this context of justice? Is it fair to assume that all charities are just? Can we take the meaning of charity and charities to be synonymous?

Sadly, in the wake of the many scandals that we have all read about and which we have already made reference to earlier in this book, the view of charities is not always as positive as we might hope. Public confidence in charities is at an all-time low according to the Charity Commission for England and Wales.[11] As I write, the case of the now defunct Kids Company charity is being fought in the High Court, with accusations of salacious spending and insufficient accountability being made against its leaders and trustees.[12] If such accusations are found to be true, how can this be characteristic of a just charity?

Equally, we have heard of other failures of charities to operate in a manner that upholds justice, safe working practices and cultures that challenge harmful behaviours. What has become known as the 'Oxfam scandal' is just one such example. Of course, Oxfam as an international charity were not alone in discovering the abuse, exploitation and harassment of their beneficiaries by their own workers. In the months that followed the uncovering of widespread exploitation, abuse and harassment across the aid and development sector, I (Justin) was invited to join an expert panel to advise the government on the key issues surrounding safeguarding in the sector from a faith-based perspective. There would have been no need for such a group had all the charities found to be operating in this way been just rather than complicit in abusive practices. So what exactly does a just charity look like?

Charities as advocates and campaigners

Our concept of a *just charity* needs to go beyond acting justly in our programmes and operations, to tackling systemic injustice through advocacy and campaigns.

Thankfully, in the UK, it is accepted, if not encouraged, that charities should be active as advocates and campaigners.[13] This tradition is long-established. If we apply all we have explored about *just leadership* to just charities, we will see organizations speaking up and putting the needs of others at the heart of their activities: whether that is campaigning for legislative change, observation and consistent application of existing law, or decision-making of local and central government to name a few.

The definition of advocacy is simply to speak up for, or on behalf of a person, cause or course of action. This returns us to a fundamental principle of what *just leadership* is all about. If our organizations or charities are not the vehicle through which we are empowered to raise our voices in the public square for the common good, they are arguably not *just charities* at all.

Bringing broader public attention to matters of injustice should be fundamental to the existence of charities. Indeed, the establishment of many charities has been as a direct response to the many injustices seen in society. They are necessary in the fight, bringing focus and resources to the multitude of challenges facing our world today, as suggested by the Association of Chief Executives of Voluntary Organisations (ACEVO):

Charities do not arise out of a vacuum. They are a response to an identified need in society, be it a social injustice, health problem or an environmental issue. Not all of these needs can ever totally be resolved but all charities work towards a vision in which their charitable aims are met.[14]

Let's not be confused by thinking that these advocacy and campaigning efforts are always required to be political. Without question, for some, the need to be at the heart of politics and policy making is key to their success. For many, however, it is simply the desire and tenacity to keep digging-in to ensure the needs of the disadvantaged, disaffected and disconnected remain on the agenda and are met with services, support and a continuing measure of dignity. Politics may therefore be the manner in which these injustices are approached, but politics is not the end game – it is about people, community and society. The role of a just charity is to consistently and courageously stand in the gap:

The problem which divides people today is not a political problem; it is a social one. It is a matter of knowing which will get the upper hand, the spirit of selfishness or the spirit of sacrifice; whether society will go for ever-increasing enjoyment and profit, or for everyone devoting themselves to the common good . . .We must get in between these two groups, at least to reduce the impact if we cannot stop it.[15]

Charity and justice go hand-in-hand

In modern day British society we still see many Christian organizations at the forefront of combatting a wide variety of social concerns, challenges and injustices; examples include Christians Against Poverty (CAP), Transforming Lives for Good (TLG), International Justice Mission (IJM), Hope for Justice, Safe Families, Home for Good, Kintsugi Hope, The Trussell Trust, Restored and thirtyone:eight, among many others. We don't intend this to be seen as some sort of exclusive or exhaustive list as there are many, many others working in other areas of social concern inspired by their Christian faith and their pursuit of justice. However, these and others should inspire us to keep going, to maintain our focus and avoid the many distractions that might pull us away from leading justly towards a more just society, whether in churches, charities, businesses or other settings. As Ken Costa reminds us, there is a work to be done if we are ready and willing:

> This is our challenge today: to see our callings in the context of the wider world. We are not called to sit apart from the world, but to engage with it in the light of Christ . . . This is the supreme work of the Spirit of God. But he stirs only where he sees servants ready to work at healing a broken society.[16]

You see charity and justice go hand-in-hand. They draw their inspiration and reason for being from the same place. Acting justly is, without doubt, a clear and high calling, and charity may be the vehicle that helps us get there.

This is what the LORD Almighty said: 'Administer true justice; show mercy and compassion to one another.'
(Zechariah 7.9)

Reflections

1 If you had the same mindset as Christ in your relationships, what difference might it make to the way you relate to others and the way you think of charity?
2 Are you confident about the mission God is calling you to – how did God call you?
3 Do you see the hallmarks of a just charity in the organization you lead or are a part of – how is *just leadership* encouraged and given a platform through its purpose and ethos?

Justice is the state that exists when there is equity, balance, and harmony in relationships and in society. Injustice is the state that exists when unjust people do violence to peace and shalom and create inequity, imbalance, and dissonance.

KEN WYTSMA[1]

18

Just business

SIMON BARRINGTON

Any study of ethics recognizes that it is the workplace where we tend to feel injustices most personally and most acutely – if only because it is a place where we spend most of our leadership time.

As the Josephson Institute of Business Ethics states:

> When money, competition, and pride are at stake, both petty and serious unfairness are common — taking credit for another's work, shifting blame, inequitable allocation of workload, promotions of the less competent for political reasons. And then there are all those double standards. Some do less work, and what they do isn't good. They come in late, miss deadlines, and make mistakes. Yet they get the same raise as you. The company has strict rules, but when bosses do something you would get fired for, they receive only a slap on the wrist, if that.[2]

Underlying this are core concerns about distributive justice – the fairness of particular decisions or allocations. As Demuijnck argues in *Duties of Justice in Business*:

> Traders are accused of receiving indecently high bonuses; CEOs benefit from shockingly high packages on dismissal – the 'golden parachutes'; the announcement of a massive lay-off boosts share value on the stock markets; and multinationals are said to exploit supplier companies and, indirectly, their workers in emerging countries. The list of complaints is endless. However, justice, more particularly distributive justice, is a complex issue. Moreover, the

scope and the relevance of the different principles of distributive justice in the business world is not obvious.[3]

Coupled with these concerns about distributive justice, there is a growing sense that the banking crisis, as well as wider concerns about capitalism, are not simply flaws in one sector of the economy but wider indicators of systemic injustice.

As the World Economic Forum states:

> Call it what you like: conscious capitalism, responsible capitalism, ethical capitalism – the better way to practice capitalism is to move the needle towards creating long-term socio-economic and environmental value: a business model with a higher purpose, where businesses build deep, trust-based relationships with their customers, employees, suppliers, investors and society.

> The bottom line benefits too from this kind of ethical, values-driven capitalism. Businesses adopting this model attract more customers, reduce operating costs through energy efficiency and lower waste, boost employee loyalty and enjoy engaged workforces that share the corporate vision, aspirations and goals.[4]

There is a greater focus here on procedural justice – the process by which a decision is made – and changes to the structures and operations of business than on the decisions themselves, and that will also be the focus of our approach to ensuring *just business*. We will focus on the changes to the underlying ethics, processes and relationships that ensure a fair and *just business* rather than on discussions about the distribution of wealth.

The relational purpose of companies

It's no accident that many of our businesses are limited companies. The word and concept has had a deep and powerful meaning which in a capitalist society has mainly been lost.

The English word *company* has its origins in the French term *compagnie* (first recorded in 1150), meaning a 'society, friendship, intimacy; body of soldiers', which in turn came from the Latin word *companio* ('one who eats bread with you').

And so right at the heart of our business life and history we have the concept of a depth of relationship with one another that has a common purpose, a common hospitality, a common sense of what is right and a desire to 'be in relationship with one another'.

We saw in Chapter 1 how in creation we see a good and just God creating a good and just world. The relationships between God, people and creation were as they should be. With the Fall, however, sin entered into God's good creation. Sin breaks our relationship with God, and it also breaks our relationship with each other, with ourselves, and with creation. Injustice is a result of that sin – both personal sin, and systemic sin – a result of those broken relationships.

Restoring broken relationships – restoring the sense that we are companions on a purposeful journey – is at the heart of recapturing a sense of business that is just, that does the right thing.

I believe that we are on the cusp of businesses beginning to grasp that there is a way that business works, a way that brings wholeness, authentic relationships and justice and that enables businesses to be more sustainable, more holistic and more relevant.[5] A way that we understand was ordained by God and that can be redeemed.

As I wrote in *Unleashed: The ACTS Church today*:

> . . . the environment in businesses is changing and waking up to these realities: that the current system is broken and is not working. Frederick Laloux, a mainstream business author who has a huge following, in his book *Re-inventing Organizations*, describes the future of business as being (1) wholehearted, (2) purposeful and (3) self-managed. This new way of working recognises the change in order of 'seeking' in our lives. Recognition, success, wealth and belonging are no longer the primary things that are sought after. Rather, 'we pursue a life well lived, and the consequences might just be recognition, success, wealth and love'.

> In this context the new watchwords of business are relationship, honesty, integrity, authenticity, wholeness and purpose.[6]

And I might add the result of all this is . . . justice.

It is our contention that a more relational company is a more just company, a more just business. As the Relationships Foundation explains:

> A Relational Company would cease to be an agglomeration of individual goals, which are often competing and primarily financial. Rather, the stakeholders in a Relational Company get to know each other and become, in a limited sense, a community, characterised like all communities by conversation, a shared story, mutual respect, an alignment of interests and a common direction. In this context all stakeholders would take greater responsibility for the impact of their actions on others, increase their ability to achieve their individual goals, and increase the wider and long-term benefit of companies to society.[7]

A right relationship with ourselves

We saw in Chapter 3 that this all starts with a right relationship with ourselves. A focus on developing a 'just me'. We won't go over all that ground again here, but just to emphasize that the start of just business is a deep inner work of character development in ourselves that enables us to look out for the interests of others, build long-lasting, trusting and mutually beneficial relationships and ultimately community.

If my focus is what can I get out, what can I gain, what can I lose, what can I profit from – then inevitably our attempts to build just businesses will fail at the first hurdle.

At the core of a just business therefore is a passion and a desire to teach individuals to love and trust themselves and to take joy in their interdependence. As David Brooks writes in his bestseller, *The Road to Character*:

> A mature person possesses a settled unity of purpose. The mature person has moved from fragmentation to centredness, has achieved a state in which restlessness is over, the confusion about the meaning and purpose of life is calmed. The mature person can make decisions without relying on the negative and positive reactions from admirers

or detractors because the mature person has steady criteria to determine what is right. That person has said a multitude of noes for the sake of a few overwhelming yeses.[8]

He continues: 'There's a joy in a life filled with interdependence with others, in a life filled with gratitude, reverence and admiration.'

A right relationship with others

As we have already seen, acting justly requires that we – having developed a sense of rightness with ourselves – really begin to see other people as whole people. Edgar and Peter Schein articulate the following attributes of the humble leader who sees others as whole people:

> This kind of relationship implies a deeper level of trust and openness in terms of (1) making and honouring commitments and promises to each other, (2) agreeing to not undermine each other or harm what we have agreed to do, and (3) agreeing not to lie to each other or withhold information relevant to our task.[9]

It involves building trust and 'learning together', being willing to share challenges and failures, walking humbly and being prepared to admit when we get it wrong.

It involves moving from a model of 'heroic' leader, that is about 'me' and 'transactions', to a justice-based leader that is focused on 'we' and 'you'.

Underlying all of this is a desire to love our neighbour as we love ourselves. To build God-honouring relationships that are an outworking of the great commandment.

All this mirrors the notion of 'togetherness' that Justin spoke of in the earlier chapter on 'holding ourselves accountable'.

As David Brooks continues:

> [This] tender character-building strategy is based on the idea that we can't always resist our desires, but we can change and reorder our desires by focusing on our higher loves. Focus on your love for your children. Focus on your love of country. Focus on your love of

the poor and downtrodden. Focus on your love of your hometown or alma mater. To sacrifice for such things is sweet. It feels good to serve your beloved. Giving becomes cheerful giving because you are so eager to see the things you love prosper and thrive.[10]

This focus on building mutually beneficial relationships extends not only to our colleagues at the next desk, or on a Zoom call, but also to the whole of the eco-system in which we work.

A right relationship with creation

This eco-system involves the whole of creation with which we interact. From natural resources to the people and processes, policies and practices that utilize them. Just as treating our fellow humans in a dehumanized way is unjust, failing to steward the creation for the common good is also unjust. As Chris Wright explains in his book *The Mission of God*:

> Creation care embodies justice because environmental action is a form of defending the weak against the strong, the defenceless against the powerful, the violated against the attacker, the voiceless against the stridency of the greedy. And these too are features of the character of God as expressed in his exercise of justice.[11]

He continues:

> For the Church to get involved with issues of environmental protection it must be prepared to tackle the forces of greed and economic power, to confront vested interests and political machination, to recognise that more is at stake than just being kind to animals and nice to people . . . It must be willing for the long, hard road that the struggle for justice and compassion in a fallen world demands.

Ruth Valerio, Global Advocacy and Influencing Director at Tearfund puts this in a very practical way:

We need to take steps in our own churches, but we also need to engage in advocacy, in speaking up about the big issues and the policies and practices coming from business and corporations. Whatever the future holds, I know that God has created us in order to look after everything that He has made, both humans and species.[12]

As business leaders we have a responsibility to act justly towards our people, our places and our planet. To restore right relationships between our organizations and the environment in which they are placed.

As Tom Wright puts it:

> ... the fact that God has renewed creation in Jesus and intends to renew it from top to bottom in the end should have immediate implications for our care of the planet. If someone gave you a wonderful painting to decorate your home, it wouldn't be very respectful if you used it as a dart-board, or as a chalkboard for the kids to draw on. And if someone said that didn't matter because the original artist would come one day and mend it and clean it up, you might think that wasn't the point. But that's how we have often treated God's good creation.[13]

In the next section we look at some of the ways that businesses can start to put justice at the centre of their agenda for individuals, groups and society at large by doing the right thing.

Doing the right thing

There are several excellent models and significant movement towards businesses becoming more just in their actions.

The Centre for Social and Economic Justice puts forward its approach to Justice-Based Management:

> Justice-Based Management seeks to balance moral values (treating people with fairness and dignity) with material value (increasing a company's productiveness and profits while enriching all members of a productive enterprise). Its three basic operating principles are:

1 Build the organization on shared ethical values — starting with respect for the dignity and worth of each person (employee, customer and supplier) — that promote the development and empowerment of every member of the group.
2 Succeed in the marketplace by delivering maximum value (higher quality at lower prices) to the customer.
3 Reward people commensurate with the value they contribute to the company — as individuals and as a team.[14]

Lily Zheng in her article for the Harvard Business Review argues that the corporate social responsibility that has become part and parcel of corporate life, does not go far enough and needs to be replaced by a sense of corporate social justice.

Corporate Social Justice is a reframing of Corporate Social Responsibility (CSR) that centres the focus of any initiative or program on the measurable, lived experiences of groups harmed and disadvantaged by society. CSR is a self-regulated framework that has no legal or social obligation for corporations to actually create positive impact for the groups they purport to help. Corporate Social Justice is a framework regulated by the trust between a company and its employees, customers, shareholders, and the broader community it touches, with the goal of explicitly doing good by all of them. Where CSR is often realized through a secondary or even vanity program tacked on to a company's main business, Corporate Social Justice requires deep integration with every aspect of the way a company functions.[15]

Karen L. Newman goes even further in her article 'The Just Organization: Creating and Maintaining Justice in Work Environments', arguing that organizations need to go beyond maximizing shareholder wealth in order to create more ethical, justice-based environments:

Put another way, corporate goals that include an emphasis on customer needs, employee needs, and community citizenship are likely to be more ethical because the organization has 'humanized' its goals and its agenda. It is much easier to be unethical when the victim is faceless.

Her emphasis, once again is on prioritizing the focus on the lives of real people and relationship:

> Organizations with humanized goals are more likely to have ethical work climates and are therefore more likely to be characterized by perceptions of justice for all. Whether people are in fact treated with justice is, unfortunately, another matter."[16]

The Josephson Institute of Business Ethics argues that organizations can move towards a more just and ethical environment by ensuring that they have a set of 'principles of fairness'.

This is an interesting way of addressing the justice challenge, as:

> Fairness as a corporate doctrine can be applied to all stakeholders and define a culture of trust and openness, with all the corresponding benefits, in marketing, advertising, board development, client relations, and so on. It is also an effective way of integrating business ethics into the organization so ethics is no longer seen as the responsibility solely of the compliance department or legal team."[17]

The principles of fairness which they articulate are these.

- Treat all people equitably based on their merits and abilities and handle all essentially similar situations similarly and with consistency.
- Make all decisions on appropriate criteria, without undue favouritism or improper prejudice.
- Never blame or punish people for what they did not do, and appropriately sanction those who violate moral obligations or laws.
- Promptly and voluntarily correct personal and institutional mistakes and improprieties.
- Do not take unfair advantage of people's mistakes or ignorance.

- Fully consider the rights, interests and perspectives of all stakeholders, approach judgements with open-minded impartiality (setting aside prejudices and predispositions), conscientiously gather and verify facts, provide critical stakeholders with an opportunity to explain or clarify and carefully evaluate the information.[18]

The Relational Business Charter

The most comprehensive approach that I have seen to implementing a more human, more relational approach that can lead to a more ethical environment that is imbued with justice, is the Relational Business Charter, from the Relationships Foundation at Cambridge University.

The Relational Business Charter assesses whether the conditions for effective relationships are being fostered. These include issues of communication, time, knowledge, power and purpose within a relationship and their capacity to foster trust, understanding, accountability, loyalty, respect, fairness and other relational outcomes. Consultation with a wide range of professions and businesses has resulted in the following proposed principles.

1 **Set relational goals** The company includes a relational business objective in its constitution, and demonstrates the commitment to implement it, providing appropriate training to investors, directors and employees.
2 **Create stakeholder dialogue** Dialogue is promoted among all significant stakeholder groups, through regular face-to-face meetings and, where that is not possible, through regular online communication.
3 **Demand shareholder transparency** There is direct and transparent (named) ownership of a significant proportion (perhaps 25 per cent) of the shares by individuals (or family trusts).
4 **Encourage long-term ownership** A high proportion of the shares are owned on a long-term basis (which may be encouraged by issuing additional shares to long-term shareholders).
5 **Safeguard work–life balance** There is evidence of management having respect for the interests of employees (for example, with regard

to length of working hours, unsocial hours and other employment conditions).

6 **Lower pay differentials** The dignity of all employees is respected by minimizing remuneration differentials within the business (taking, for example, a 20:1 ratio between top and bottom as a benchmark).

7 **Build supplier partnerships** Suppliers are treated fairly and with respect, paid promptly and given support to develop their businesses.

8 **Respect customers and communities** Customers and the local community are treated fairly and their concerns are respected (such as with regard to service provided and payment terms).

9 **Promote financial stability** The risk of company financial instability is minimized to protect the company and its stakeholders (assessed with reference to debt to equity ratios and/or levels of interest cover).

10 **Fulfil social obligations** Obligations to wider society are fulfilled, assessed with reference to the percentage of profits paid in tax in the country where those profits are earned and also the percentage of profits spent on corporate social responsibility.[19]

Reflection

1 How do the processes, procedures, ethics and relationships in your organization support effective justice-focused activities?

2 What changes might you need to make in your relationships with yourself and others to make a greater impact for justice in your organization?

3 How might you embed the practice of fairness more deeply into your organizational culture and ethos?

A society that wishes and intends to remain at the service of the human being at every level is a society that has the common good – the good of all people and of the whole person – as its primary goal.[1]

19

Just society

SIMON BARRINGTON AND JUSTIN HUMPHREYS

So far, we have navigated the landscape of the characteristics of leaders who live justly – who are secure in their identity, walking humbly with God and who, out of that, are demonstrating generosity, acting courageously, practising proximity, hearing voices from the outside, speaking out, walking with victims and survivors, managing power well, holding themselves accountable to others, tackling conflict and making change happen.

We've also then been able to see how these characteristics can be applied to create just businesses, just churches and just charities. These are organizations that have the stewardship of right relationships at the core of who they are and are determined to do the right thing in every case to ensure relationships flourish and people thrive.

We want to turn now, though, to thinking about wider society. What does justice look like as leaders lead justly and organizations act justly?

Our prayer and dream is that the impact of 'just leaders' working within 'just organizations' can go some way to having an impact on the rest of society with a justice perspective. Certainly, we see this as a core and fundamental part of the mission of the Church – not that it may only be a 'just Church' for the sake of itself – although that is important – but also a 'just Church' in its actions and interactions with the whole of society, such that it reflects the very nature and character of God's love for all.

But what does that vision of a 'just society' look like? It's a topic that has occupied the thoughts of many political leaders, religious leaders, theologians and sociologists over the centuries and with renewed vigour and interest in recent years.

In some ways it is much easier to describe what an unjust society looks like, partly because we inhabit the reality of seeing broken relationships, an unfair distribution of wealth and power, the marginalization of groups and the abuse and victimization of individuals on a daily basis.

It's hard to unsee what we see, but how do we envision a new reality of a 'just society' brought about by 'just leaders' and 'just organizations'?

Alternative visions

While he was the Minister of Justice, prior to his election as the fifteenth Canadian Prime Minister in 1968, Pierre Trudeau defined his vision of a 'just society':

> The Just Society will be one in which the rights of minorities will be safe from the whims of intolerant majorities. The Just Society will be one in which those regions and groups which have not fully shared in the country's affluence will be given a better opportunity. The Just Society will be one where such urban problems as housing and pollution will be attacked through the application of new knowledge and new techniques. The Just Society will be one in which our Indian and Inuit populations will be encouraged to assume the full rights of citizenship through policies which will give them both greater responsibility for their own future and more meaningful equality of opportunity. The Just Society will be a united Canada, united because all of its citizens will be actively involved in the development of a country where equality of opportunity is ensured, and individuals are permitted to fulfil themselves in the fashion they judge best ... On the never-ending road to perfect justice we will, in other words, succeed in creating the most humane and compassionate society possible.[2]

The driving themes of equal opportunity, unity, inclusion and sharing in the country's affluence were core to Trudeau's vision of human flourishing in a just society and there is much to be applauded here and recognized as embodying Christian values.

It is certainly a vision that is hard to attain, demanding as it does a sense of 'looking out for the other' which has been undermined by a singular focus in most Western economies on individual development and the market economy.

The Archbishop of Canterbury Justin Welby extends our thinking further as he takes up the theme of a just society in the William Temple Foundation Annual Lecture he gave in May 2019.

The Christian faith puts social affairs within the overarching framework (2nd Peter) of a loving God, a God of justice, mercy and redemption, demonstrated most powerfully in Jesus Christ. It places our relationships with each other in the context of our common humanity – so greatly needed in these times when divisions exist both within and between societies . . .

They lift it [social justice] into a framework of love and faith, as we have respect for the human dignity of all people as made in the image of God. Isaiah 58 talks of the hypocrisy of fasting on the sabbath, whilst exploiting our workers and quarrelling with one another. The kind of fasting God has chosen is not piety on a Sunday, it is 'to loose the chains of injustice and untie the cords of the yoke, to set the oppressed free and break every yoke' (NIV). Social justice is a fundamental part of the radical message of the Gospel. When prosperity and justice go hand in hand, every part of society benefits, and they should be seen in the community life of the church.

Even in our understanding of what exactly *social justice* is, however, we must be careful not to compartmentalize our efforts in a singular direction and thereby lose the bigger picture of what we are called to:

When we think a single shard of the mosaic of justice describes the whole, it's as if we're cataloguing one particular butterfly and assuming we've understood every other species that swoops and sways through the sky.[3]

In other words, there remains a danger that the pursuit of justice only partially inhabits our lives; we may be active in this area, but not that, either intentionally or unwittingly. In missing the need to understand how justice should permeate our entire lives, we risk a hypocrisy that only serves to undermine the credibility of our efforts in the eyes of wider society.

Welby takes up this theme:

> We need to love the whole more than ourselves. There is too much of a tendency in our world, and even in the church, that we would sometimes prefer to rule over the ruins than to serve in the intact structure. As Desmond Tutu wrote, 'We are different so that we can know our need of one another, for no one is ultimately self-sufficient.'[4]

Welby speaks prophetically to the heart of the matter: 'We need to love the whole more than ourselves'. This turns our cultural values and norms upside down, resetting our priorities. A call to ubuntu – as we saw in Chapter 2 – to proclaim from the rooftops and to embed in our life and work the heart cry of 'I am because we are'.

The common good

From the era of ancient Greece through to contemporary philosophy, many philosophers, thinkers and theologians have articulated this desire for a society that is not just derived from a collection of individuals living independently, but envisioned as connected citizens deeply engaged and interdependent in their relationships and lives. They have called this the common good.

Although definitions vary, the common good has always included the possibility that the public good – such as education and justice – need a coming together in action and participation in the public square that is not possible without a common vision of interdependence.

This wrestle with the common good is deep in our thinking as Christians as well. As Andrew Bradstock points out, the Book of Common Prayer asks its readers to ask God to 'give wisdom to all in authority; and direct this and every nation in the ways of justice and of peace; that we may honour one another and seek the common good'.[5]

Catholic social teaching has also sought to explain its sense of the meaning of the common good, with the Second Vatican Council articulating: 'According to its primary and broadly accepted sense, *the common good* indicates "the sum total of social conditions which allow people, either as groups or as individuals, to reach their fulfilment more fully and more easily".[6]

The common good seems to have been part and parcel of early Church life as well:

> They devoted themselves to the apostles' teaching and to fellowship, to the breaking of bread and to prayer. Everyone was filled with awe at the many wonders and signs performed by the apostles. All the believers were together and had everything in common. They sold property and possessions to give to anyone who had need. Every day they continued to meet together in the temple courts. They broke bread in their homes and ate together with glad and sincere hearts, praising God and enjoying the favour of all the people. And the Lord added to their number daily those who were being saved. (Acts 2.42–47)

The Greek word *koinonia*, usually translated as 'communion' or 'fellowship' and used in this passage, gives us another insight into the Christian understanding of the common good. There is a rich and deep community here: focused on serving one another, focused on loving one another, focused on including those in need, focused on enjoying one another's company, focused on interdependent relationship with one another and with God.

Also, as Jesus said, 'A new command I give you: love one another. As I have loved you, so you must love one another. By this everyone will know that you are my disciples, if you love one another' (John 13.34–35).

The common good in reality

Michael Sandel, Professor of Political Philosophy at Harvard University and author of *The Tyranny of Merit: What's become of the common good?*

suggests four elements of society that need to be challenged in order to embrace working for the common good and creating a just society.[7]

1 **We need to call people to citizenship, sacrifice and service** Images of individual prosperity and flourishing at the expense of others need to be replaced with a common vision of service and sacrifice. A clear articulation of what it means to be a citizen who stands in solidarity with others who are less well-off and works collaboratively with a sense of mutual responsibility.

2 **We need to understand the moral limits of markets** Sandel argues that market thinking has extended into areas that it was never intended to influence – such as healthcare, education, transport, justice and welfare, and that market forces are ill equipped to produce outcomes that are for the common good in these areas. He calls for a public debate on the moral limits of markets and the areas and sectors that market thinking should not be applied to.

3 **We need to tackle inequality** Inequality leads to a lack of civic engagement for the common good. As individuals become wealthier, they retreat from public spaces and civic engagement to the exclusivity of private members' clubs, private jets and private schools. An example would be in Los Angeles where the Metro system has no advertising, basically because the target demographic for advertisers is not the demographic who use the Metro. Advertisers' target demographic are those overhead in cars and planes and helicopters. This economic impact also has social and civic impacts.

4 **We need to engage morally and politically** Sandel argues that we have retreated from public discourse on moral issues because of our pluralistic society. We have avoided the various convictions that our fellow citizens bring to public life and we need to attend to them more directly. Only in this way can there be a constructive dialogue about what the common good looks like. We may find that we have more to bring to this dialogue when we stand together on issues of justice than we first imagined. For example, the Abrahamic Faiths Peace-making Initiative in Los Angeles is a group of American clergy and religious activists who advocate peace-making as an essential and defining mandate of three faith traditions – Judaism, Christianity and Islam.

By bringing together a collection of each faith's relevant teachings, they aim to contribute an authentic and substantive religious voice to the current peace movement, to activate people of faith to insist on peaceful solutions to local, national and global conflicts, and, in particular, to end the war and US occupation in Iraq.

Some examples of working for the common good

There is no doubt that Aneurin Bevin had working for the common good in mind when he set out his original vision for the National Health Service – sorry, *our* National Health Service – in 1948, which was to provide medical care, free at point of need to everyone in the UK: 'no society can legitimately call itself civilized if a sick person is denied medical aid because of lack of means'.

Evidence of the love and respect for our NHS has never been plainer to see than in the first five months of lockdown during the COVID-19 crisis, from April to August 2020. Every Thursday night at 8 p.m., the general admiration for healthcare workers right across the UK was shown by people standing on their doorsteps and clapping, mainly, but also banging saucepans, playing musical instruments and displaying posters and ornaments to express their profound thanks to a beloved institution.

The sense that people in the UK wanted to maintain our NHS for all the people, all of the time, has never been more strongly expressed, nor has the sense that the NHS was indeed working for the common good. The social pressure to reward health workers well, to fund the NHS well and to keep the vision of a service for all, free at point of need, to fulfil the common good has also never been greater.

Another example of working for the common good is Muhammad Yunus's efforts to reform the banking system in Central Asia, to make it accessible to the poor. Often called 'Banker to the Poor', Yunus set up the Grameen Bank in Bangladesh initially and pioneered the concept of micro-loans and micro-finance. He identified that traditional banks had been reluctant to lend money to anyone unable to give some form of security. Grameen Bank, however, works on the assumption that even the poorest of the poor can manage their own financial affairs and development, given suitable conditions. In this way, through micro-loans, Yunus opened up the banking system for the common good, thereby altering the existing systems of economic injustice.

Risk everything to do the right thing

There is no question that there is much to do in bringing this pursuit of justice to society through our leadership. This is big! It would be a tragedy to have to say that this is 'the next big thing' because that would clearly indicate it has yet to take its proper place in our society. But maybe that's where we still are to a large extent.

Look around you. Who do you see that is inspiring the kind of leadership we have been discussing in the pages of this book? I guess you might see a few people, but you probably can't see too many. At least, it would seem hard at times to see clearly those just leaders rising above the waves of the many others who have a different agenda in mind. But don't be disheartened. Hasn't this always been the case? Nothing good (or just) ever came easy, right?

We want to encourage you to exercise every ounce of agency you have to rise above the waves and sail forwards to act justly – in all areas of your life and ministry. Yes, it's a tough call, but it is one that has literally life-changing properties. That call to act justly has been ringing clear for millennia and its chimes are ringing louder than ever right now. Sometimes, we have to be that person who swims against the tide, puts the needs of others ahead of our own and can be seen to be shouting the unpopular message from the rooftops to influence the common or greater good. In the conclusion to his book *Consequential Leadership*, Mac Pier reflects on the courage and determination of Abraham Lincoln as an example of what it can take to make the change happen:

> On February 27, 1860, Lincoln gave his 'Cooper Union' speech in downtown Manhattan. In it, he declared his position against slavery and its expansion into new territories. The speech galvanised northern voters to support his candidacy, and Lincoln leveraged the influence of New York City to electrify the nation. The Cooper Union speech had changed the world.[8]

Clearly, Lincoln is not the only example we could have given and, in some ways, his story is not dissimilar to that of Yunus, who was also instrumental in making changes and opening up a new way for society. Lincoln spoke against the popular vote and prevailing view. He galvanized the voters to support change. He chose to risk everything to do the right thing – to see justice prevail. It was the start of something new, but certainly was not the end. Neither did it pave the way for all such changes to roll in without any further challenge as we all know. But it was the start and a start is what we can all make – in our church, our charity, company or community. Just in case you need a reminder of somebody else who made that same self-sacrificing journey for the common good, look no further than Jesus himself.

The glory of God and justice

As we come to the end of this journey, we hope that you are inspired to see your own leadership transformed, to see your own organization – charity, church or business – transformed and to see society transformed. There is no doubt that we will all need to be reminded continually to be hopeful and patient as we pursue these goals, which demand our intentional focus and energy.

As we end, though, let's remind ourselves of why we seek the common good, why we seek for justice, why we want to be just leaders.

We care about justice because justice is who God *is* and what God *does*.
We care about justice because Jesus does.
We care about justice because God calls us to act justly.

Because of that, we long for God's inbreaking justice. As N. T. Wright puts it:

The whole point of the Gospels is that the coming of God's kingdom on earth as in heaven is precisely not the imposition of an alien and dehumanizing tyranny, but rather the confrontation of alien and dehumanizing tyrannies with the news of a God – the God recognized in Jesus – who is radically different from them all, and whose inbreaking justice aims at rescuing and restoring genuine humanness.[9]

And we know that when that inbreaking justice comes, then there is wholeness and healing and mercy and grace and a righting of wrongs. There is a shalom and a flourishing. There is a sense of being us rather than me. There is a coming of the kingdom of God.

David Hollenbach, in his article for the Berkley Centre for Religion, Peace and World Affairs at Georgetown University, entitled 'The glory of God and the global common good: Solidarity in a turbulent world', argues that the current turbulence in society requires a strengthened commitment to justice and to the common good.

The glory of God will shine forth in its full splendour when our many relationships with each other and with the earth are brought to fulfilment in union with God and with each other in God. As we move toward that fulfilment, we are called to labour in hope for a fuller achievement of the common good that will make the beauty of God's love and justice more visible in our world.

We both desire, more than anything, that the beauty of God's love and justice will become more visible in our world, that God's inbreaking justice will be evident in our lives, in our families, in our communities, in our organizations and in the world for the glory of the God, who we love and serve.

Reflections

1   What does a 'just society' look like to you and how do you encourage others to see what you see?
2   What steps can you take to identify, prioritize and pursue the common good over and above the immediate goals that you or your organization may have?
3   How do our actions in fighting for the common good reflect the will and heart of God to those around us, such that he is glorified?

References

Preface

1 Office for National Statistics (2020) 'Deaths involving COVID-19 by local area and socioeconomic deprivation: Deaths occurring between 1 March and 17 April 2020' (available online at: <www.ons.gov.uk/peoplepopulationandcommunity/birthsdeathsandmarriages/deaths/bulletins/deathsinvolvingcovid19bylocalareasanddeprivation/deaths occurringbetween1marchand17april>, accessed 4 May 2020).
2 Institute for Fiscal Studies (2020) 'Are some ethnic groups more vulnerable to COVID-19 than others?' (available online at: <www.ifs.org.uk/inequality/chapter/are-some-ethnic-groups-more-vulnerable-to-covid-19-than-others>, accessed 4 May 2020).
3 Sally Weale (2020) 'Sharp rise in number of calls to ChildLine over coronavirus', *The Guardian*, 27 March (available online at: <www.theguardian.com/world/2020/mar/27/sharp-rise-in-number-of-calls-to-childline-over-coronavirus>, accessed 20 October 2020).

1 Just God

1 Tom Wright (2011) *Simply Christian* (London: SPCK), p. 117.
2 Gary Haugen (2009) *Good News about Injustice: A witness of courage in a hurting world* (Nottingham: IVP), p. 84.
3 Bryant L. Myers (1999) *Walking with the Poor: Principles and practices of transformational development* (Maryknoll, NY: Orbis), p. 64.
4 Ken Wytsma (2013) *Pursuing Justice: The call to live and die for bigger things* (Nashville, TN: Thomas Nelson), p. 19.
5 Just Love (n.d.) 'Theology of justice' (available online at: <https://justloveuk.com/about-us/theology-of-justice>, accessed 10 November 2020).
6 Mike Kelly (2018) 'The justice series: The beginning of justice' (available online at: <www.biblica.com/articles/the-beginning-of-justice>, accessed September 2020).
7 Glenn Smith (2012) 'Shalom', in Mac Pier, *Consequential Leadership* (Downers Grove, IL: InterVarsity Press), pp. 68–79.

8 Ken Wytsma (2015) *The Grand Paradox: The messiness of life, the mystery of God and the necessity of faith* (Nashville, TN: Thomas Nelson), p. 45.

9 Mike Kelly (2018) 'The justice series: The story of Israel' (available online at: <www.biblica.com/articles/story-of-israel>, accessed September 2020).

10 Tim Keller (2010) *Generous Justice: How God's grace makes us just* (London: Hodder & Stoughton), p. 40.

11 Ben Lindsay (2019) *We Need to Talk about Race: Understanding the black experience in white majority churches* (London: SPCK), p. 93.

12 Just Love (n.d.) 'Theology of justice'.

13 Christopher J. H. Wright (2006) *The Mission of God: Unlocking the Bible's grand narrative* (Nottingham: IVP), p. 312.

14 Wright, *The Mission of God*, p. 314.

15 Tom Wright (n.d.) 'Beginning to think about the new creation' (available online at: <www.ntwrightonline.org/beginning-to-think-about-the-new-creation>, accessed September 2020).

16 BBC News (n.d.) 'Beslan school siege' (available online at: <http://news.bbc.co.uk/1/shared/spl/hi/world/04/russian_s/html/7.stm>, accessed 5 March 2021).

2 Just me

1 Peter Gill (2010) *Famine and Foreigners in Ethiopia Since Live Aid* (Oxford: Oxford University Press), p. 44 (available online at: <https://sahistory.org.za/sites/default/files/file%20uploads%20/peter_gill_famine_and_foreigners_ethiopia_sincebook4you.pdf>, accessed 8 March 2021).

2 Christopher J. H. Wright (2017) 'Made for mission: What does being made in the image of God mean for our understanding of mission?', in Krish Kandiah, Hannah J. Swithinbank and David Westlake (eds), 'Made in the Image of God' (Tearfund), pp. 19–34 (available online at: <https://learn.tearfund.org/~/media/files/tilz/churches/integral_mission/2017-tearfund-made-in-the-image-of-god-essays-en.pdf>, accessed 4 May 2020).

3 Andy Crouch (2017) 'Restoring the image: Idolatry, injustice and the image of the invisible God', in Krish Kandiah, Hannah J. Swithinbank and David Westlake (eds), 'Made in the Image of God' (Tearfund), pp. 35–43 (available online at: <https://learn.tearfund.org/~/media/files/tilz/churches/integral_mission/2017-tearfund-made-in-the-image-of-god-essays-en.pdf>, accessed 4 May 2020)

4 *Mere Christianity* by CS Lewis © copyright CS Lewis Pte Ltd 1942, 1943, 1944, 1952. Used with permission.

5 Dallas Willard (2012) *Renovation of the Heart: Putting on the character of Christ* (10th Anniversary Edition) (Colorado Springs, CO: NavPress), p. 39.

6 Brené Brown (2017) *Braving the Wilderness: The quest for true belonging and the courage to stand alone* (London: Ebury). Kindle edition, location 697.

7 Tim Keller (2010) *Generous Justice: How God's grace makes us just* (London: Hodder & Stoughton).

8 Eric Berne (1961) *Transactional Analysis in Psychotherapy* (New York: Ballantine Books).

9 Patrick Regan OBE (2019) 'Wellbeing groups: Discovering treasure in life's scars', Kintsugi Hope (available online at: <www.kintsugihope.com/files/groups/KHWG%20-%20Leaders%20Guide.pdf>, accessed 2 March 2021).

10 Samaritan's Purse (2020) 'Let my heart be broken by the things that break the heart of God', 25 January (available online at: <https://samaritanspurse.org/article/let-my-heart-be-broken-by-the-things-that-break-the-heart-of-god>, accessed 24 October 2020).

3 Just us

1 J. R. R. Tolkien (1976) *The Lord of the Rings: The Return of the King* (4th edn) (London: Unwin), pp. 190–2.

2 S. R. Covey (1992) *Principle-centred Leadership* (London: Simon & Schuster), p. 58.

3 Will van der Hart and Rob Waller (2019) *The Power of Belonging: Discovering the confidence to lead with vulnerability* (Colorado Springs, CO: David C. Cook, 2019), p. 64.

4 Paul Swann (2018) *Sustaining Leadership: You are more important than your ministry* (Abingdon: BRF), p. 57.

5 Simon Barrington with Rachel Luetchford (2019) *Leading – the Millennial Way* (London: SPCK).

6 Charles Van Engen (2001) 'Towards a theology of mission partnerships', in *Missiology: An International Review*, XXIX (1), January, pp. 11–44 (available online at: <https://journals.sagepub.com/doi/abs/10.1177/009182960102900102>, accessed 10 June 2020).

7 Sonya Sachdeva, Rumen Iliev, Hamed Ekhtiari, Morteza Dehghani (2015) 'The role of self-sacrifice in moral dilemmas', *PLOS ONE*, 15 June (available online at: <https://journals.plos.org/plosone/article?id=10.1371/journal.pone.0127409>, accessed 9 October 2020).

4 Speaking up

1 Aaron O'Neill (2020) 'Number of countries where the highest position of executive power was held by a woman, in each year from 1960 to 2020', Statista, 6 April (available online at: <www.statista.com/statistics/1058345/

countries-with-women-highest-position-executive-power-since-1960>,
accessed 27 April 2020).

2 Lisa Bevere (2013) *Girls with Swords: How to carry your cross like a hero*
(Colorado Springs, CO: Waterbrook Press), p. 8.

3 United Nations (n.d.) 'Sustainable Development Goals: Goal 5: Gender
equality: Achieve gender equality and empower all women and girls' (goals
adopted in 2015) (available online at: <www.un.org/sustainabledevelopment/
gender-equality>, accessed 27 April 2020).

4 Peter Checkland and Jim Scholes (1999) *Soft Systems Methodology in Action*
(Chichester: Wiley).

5 Michel Foucault (1983) 'The meaning and evolution of the word "parrhesia":
Discourse and truth, problematization of parrhesia: Six lectures given by
Michel Foucault at the University of California at Berkeley, Oct.–Nov.
1983' (available online at: https://foucault.info/parrhesia/foucault.DT1.
wordParrhesia.en>, accessed 28 April 2020).

6 Rachael Denhollander (2018) 'The price I paid for taking on Larry
Nassar', *New York Times*, 26 January (available online at: <www.nytimes.
com/2018/01/26/opinion/sunday/larry-nassar-rachael-denhollander.html>,
accessed 28 April 2020).

7 Krish Kandiah with Justin Humphreys (2020) 'On behalf of the voiceless:
A theology of safeguarding', commissioned by thirtyone:eight (available
online at: <https://thirtyoneeight.org/about-us/why-safeguarding/theology>,
accessed 22 October 2020).

8 Lisa Oakley and Justin Humphreys (2019) *Escaping the Maze of Spiritual
Abuse: Creating healthy Christian cultures* (London: SPCK).

5 Hearing the voices from the outside

1 One Voice Collective (2020) 'Somebody please hear our voice', 5 July
(available online at: <www.youtube.com/watch?v=p_GL2-NVORg>
accessed 27 February 2021).

2 Woodrow Wilson, 'Leaders of Men', 17 June 1890 (available online at:
<https://teachingamericanhistory.org/library/document/leaders-of-men>
accessed 26 August 2020).

3 M. Scott Peck, *The Road Less Travelled* (London: Arrow Books 1990), p. 116.

4 Miguel A. De La Torre, *Reading the Bible from the Margins* (Maryknoll, NY:
Orbis Books, 2002).

5 The Lausanne Covenant (1974) (available online at: <https://lausanne.org/
content/covenant/lausanne-covenant> accessed November 2020).

6 Rick Fulwiler (2018), in Erica Hersh, 'Using effective listening to improve
leadership in environmental health and safety', Harvard School of Public

Health, 11 January (available online at: <www. hsph.harvard.edu/ecpe/listening-to-improve-leadership> accessed 27 February 2021).

7 Erin Meyer (2016) *The Culture Map* (New York: PublicAffairs).

6 Sitting with victims and survivors

1 Tom Camacho (2019) *Mining for Gold: Developing kingdom leaders through coaching* (London: IVP), p. 6.

2 Seth Godin (2008) *Tribes: We need you to lead us* (London: Piatkus), p. 47.

3 Samuel R. Chand (2015) *Leadership Pain: The classroom for growth* (Nashville, TN: Thomas Nelson), p. 15.

4 Cathy Madavan (2020) *Irrepressible: 12 principles for a courageous, resilient and fulfilling life* (London: SPCK), pp. 50–2.

5 Lisa Oakley and Justin Humphreys (2019) *Escaping the Maze of Spiritual Abuse: Creating healthy Christian cultures* (London: SPCK), p. 127.

6 Ken Wytsma (2013) *Pursuing Justice: The call to live and die for bigger things* (Nashville, TN: Thomas Nelson), p. 87.

7 Eugene H. Peterson (2012) *Tell it Slant* (Grand Rapids, MI: Eerdmans), p. 88.

8 Paula Gooder (2016) *Body: Biblical spirituality for the whole person* (London: SPCK), p. 116.

9 Patrick Regan with Liza Hoeksma (2021) *Bouncing Forwards: Notes on resilience, courage and change* (Farnham, Surrey: CWR).

7 Walking the victim's/survivor's journey

1 Thirtyone:eight, 'Safer places pledge' (2020) (available online at: <https://thirtyoneeight.org/news-and-events/pledge> accessed 20 October 2020).

2 [https://christianembassy.ca/baroness-cox-of-queensbury/]

3 Jaime Wheeler, Shared Hope International (2020) 'How not to be a square: Lessons learned walking alongside trafficking survivors' (available online at: <https://vimeo.com/442158023>, accessed 4 September 2020).

4 UNHCR (n.d.) 'Internally displaced people: Who is an internally displaced person?' (available online at: <www.unhcr.org/uk/internally-displaced-people.html>, accessed 7 March 2021.

5 UNCHR (1996) 'UNHCR publication for CIS Conference (displacement in the CIS): Conflicts in the Caucasus', 1 May (available online at: <www.unhcr.org/uk/publications/refugeemag/3b5583fd4/unhcr-publication-cis-conference-displacement-cis-conflicts-caucasus.html>, accessed 8 March 2021).

6 Wayne A. Grudem, *Systematic Theology: An introduction to biblical doctrine* (2nd edn) (London: IVP), p. 234.

7 Dan Cable (2018) 'How humble leadership really works', *Harvard Business Review*, 23 April (available online at: <https://hbr.org/2018/04/how-humble-leadership-really-works>, accessed September 2020).

8 Edgar H. Schein and Peter A. Schein (2018) *Humble Leadership: The power of relationships, openness and trust* (Oakland, CA: Berrett-Koehler), p. 24.

9 Schein, *Humble Leadership*, pp. 33–4.

10 Dale Ralph Davis (2013) *2 Samuel: Out of every adversity*, Focus on the Bible Series (Fearn, Ross-shire: Christian Focus), p. 21.

11 Will Kynes (2010) 'God's grace in the Old Testament: Considering the *hesed* of the Lord', *Knowing and Doing*, C. S. Lewis Institute, Summer (available online at: <www.cslewisinstitute.org/webfm_send/430>, accessed September 2020).

8 Practising proximity

1 Gustavo Guitierrez (2001) *A Theology of Liberation* (London: SCM Press), p. 23.

2 J. B. Phillips (2004) *Your God Is Too Small* (New York: Touchstone, 2004), p. 109.

3 Bono (2006) 'Keynote address at the 54th National Prayer Breakfast', Washington DC, 2 February (available online at: <www.americanrhetoric.com/speeches/bononationalprayerbreakfast.htm>, accessed 20 September 2020).

4 Bryant L. Myers (1999) *Walking with the Poor: Principles and practices of transformational development* (Maryknoll, NY: Orbis), p. 64.

5 Andy Crouch (2013) 'It's time to talk about power: How to recognise and use the gift that most eludes the Church', *Christianity Today*, October (available online at: <http://andy-crouch.com/articles/its_time_to_talk_about_power>, accessed 7 May 2020).

6 Forge Leadership Consultancy (2019) 'Millennial leadership' (available online at: <https://millennial-leader.com>, accessed 12 November 2020).

9 Giving generously

1 Nathaniel Hawthorne, Herman Melville, Julian Hawthorne, F. P. Stearns and G. P. Lathrop (2015) *Life and Genius of Nathaniel Hawthorne: Letters, diaries, reminiscences and extensive biographies* (Musaicum), p. 410.

2 Tim Keller (2010) *Generous Justice: How God's grace makes us just* (London: Hodder & Stoughton), p. 18.

3 Adam Grant (2013) *Give and Take: A revolutionary approach to success* (London: Orion), p. 258.

4 Adam Grant (2013) 'In the company of givers and takers', *Harvard Business Review*, April (available online at: <https://hbr.org/2013/04/in-the-company-of-givers-and-takers>, accessed 12 June 2020).

5 Tim Keller, *Generous Justice*, p. 34.

6 Izwe Nkose (2020) Lectio 365 Devotional app, daily resource for 8 June 2020, 24-7 Prayer (available online via: <www.24-7prayer.com/lectio365-resource>).

10 Managing power

1 Sara Mills (2003) *Michel Foucault* (London: Routledge), p. 47. See discussion in Sergiu Balan (2010) 'M. Foucault's view on power relations', ResearchGate, June 2010 (available online at: <www.researchgate.net/publication/321161337_M_Foucault's_View_on_Power_Relations>, accessed 8 March 2021).

2 Powercube (n.d) 'Understanding power for social change' (available online at: <www.powercube.net/other-forms-of-power/expressions-of-power>, accessed 26 August 2020).

3 Powercube, 'Understanding power for social change'.

4 Dennis Lewycky and Keitseope Nthomang (1999) *Equal Shares: Oodi weavers and the cooperative experience,* (Toronto: Between the Lines), p. 121.

5 Jo Rowlands (1997) *Questioning Empowerment: Working with women in Honduras,* Oxfam (available online at: <https://policy-practice.oxfam.org.uk/publications/questioning-empowerment-working-with-women-in-honduras-121185>, accessed 26 August 2020).

6 Blaise Pascal (1829) *Thoughts on Religion and Other Subjects* (Amerhert, MA: J. S. & C. Adams), p. 265.

11 Being courageous

1 *Hacksaw Ridge* (2016), a biographical war drama film directed by Mel Gibson, written by Andrew Knight and Robert Schenkkan, based on *The Conscientious Objector,* a 2004 documentary.

2 Frances, M. Doss (2015) *Desmond Doss Conscientious Objector: The story of an unlikely war hero* (Nampa, ID: Pacific Press), pp. 136–7.

3 Gary Haugen (2008) *Just Courage: God's great expedition for the restless Christian* (Downers Grove, IL: IVP), p. 103.

4 Lisa Oakley and Justin Humphreys (2019) *Escaping the Maze of Spiritual Abuse: Creating healthy Christian cultures* (London: SPCK), p. 136.

5 R. S. Pinto, N. Gomes, R. Radaelli, C. E. Bottom, L. E. Brown and M. Bottaro (2012) 'Effect of range of motion on muscle strength and thickness',

Journal of Strength and Conditioning Research, 26 (8), pp. 2140–5 (available online at: https://journals.lww.com/nsca-jscr/Fulltext/2012/08000/Effect_of_Range_of_Motion_on_Muscle_Strength_and.17.aspx, accessed 25 September 2020).

6 NHS (n.d.) 'Do I need to stretch before exercising?' (available online at: <www.nhs.uk/live-well/exercise/stretch-before-exercising>, accessed 25 September 2020).

12 Tackling the difficult stuff

1 Ken Blanchard, in the Foreword, to Susan Scott (2002) *Fierce Conversations: Achieving success in work and in life, one conversation at a time* (London: Hachette).

2 Theodore Roosevelt (1910) 'Citizenship in a republic', in Brené Brown (2013) *Daring Greatly: How the courage to be vulnerable transforms the way we live, love, parent, and lead* (London: Portfolio Penguin), p. 1.

3 Susan Scott (2002) *Fierce Conversations: Achieving success in work and in life, one conversation at a time* (London, Hachette Digital, Kindle edition), Kindle Location 183.

4 Brené Brown (2018) *Dare to Lead: Brave work. Tough conversations. Whole hearts* (London: Vermilion), p. 110.

5 James Kouzes and Barry Posner (2007) *The Leadership Challenge* (4th edn) (San Francisco, CA: Jossey-Bass, 2007), p. 348.

6 Richard Saundry (2019) 'Fairness, Justice and capability – repositioning conflict management', Acas discussion paper, 1 October (available online at: <www.acas.org.uk/fairness-justice-and-capability>, accessed 25 September 2020).

7 Sandra Cobbin (2015) *Leadership Resilience in Conflict* (Cambridge: Grove Books), p. 4.

8 Cobbin, *Leadership Resilience in Conflict*, p.4.

9 Alastair McKay (2016), 'Transforming conflict: Some keys for church leaders', Bridge Builders Ministries (see <www.bbministries.org.uk/wp-content/uploads/2016/04/Transforming-conflict-some-keys-for-church-leaders.pdf >, accessed 27 February 2021).

10 Speed B. Leas (1985) *Moving Your Church Through Conflict* (Plymouth: Rowman & Littlefield, Kindle edition).

11 David Cox (2007) 'The Edwin Friedman model of family systems thinking: Lessons for organizational leaders', Arkansas State University Organizational Leadership, 4 (4), 12 February (available online at: <www.peterborough-diocese.org.uk/downloads/adult-education-and-training/familysystems.pdf>, accessed 25 September 2020).

13 Making change happen

1 Eddie Gibbs (2005) *Leadership Next: Changing leaders in a changing culture* (Nottingham: IVP, 2005), p. 49.
2 Lisa Oakley and Justin Humphreys (2019) *Escaping the Maze of Spiritual Abuse: Creating healthy Christian cultures* (London: SPCK), pp. 135–7.
3 Gary Haugen, *Good News about Injustice: A witness of courage in a hurting world* (Nottingham: IVP, 2009), p. 53.
4 Justin Humphreys (2020) 'A call to righteousness: A panel discussion', at the Justice Conference UK, 21–22 February 2020, London, (unpublished). Part of a global movement encouraging thousands of Christ-followers to live out the message of Jesus and transform their communities by making justice a way of life (see <www.thejusticeconference.co.uk>, accessed 29 April 2020).
5 Thirtyone:eight (n.d.) 'Safer places pledge' (available online at: <https://thirtyoneeight.org/news-and-events/pledge>, accessed 29 April 2020).
6 Ken Wytsma (2015) *The Grand Paradox: The messiness of life, the mystery of God and the necessity of faith* (Nashville, TN: Thomas Nelson), pp. 127–8.

14 Concealing nothing

1 Thirtyone:eight (n.d.) 'Safer places pledge' (available online at: <https://thirtyoneeight.org/news-and-events/pledge>, accessed 29 April 2020).
2 Wade Mullen (2020) *Something's Not Right: Decoding the hidden tactics of abuse and freeing yourself from its power* (Carol Stream, IL: Tyndale), p. 17.
3 Graeme Cowie and Mark Sandford (2020) 'Statutory commissions of inquiry: The Inquiries Act 2005', House of Commons Library, Briefing Paper Number 06410, 8 September.
4 Jude Padfield (2019) *Hopeful Influence: A theology of Christian leadership* (London: SCM Press), p. 20.
5 Simon P. Walker (2010) *The Undefended Leader* (Carlisle: Piquant Editions), pp. 45–52.
6 Anonymous (2020) 'A Christian charity pressured me to sign a non-disclosure agreement', *Premier Christianity*, 26 August (available online at: <www.premierchristianity.com/home/a-christian-charity-pressured-me-to-sign-a-non-disclosure-agreement/3855.article>, accessed 5 October 2020).
7 Adrian Hilton (2019) 'Cheap grace and child abuse: Perhaps we need millstones hanging around a few more necks', in Janet Fife and Gilo (eds), *Letters to a Broken Church* (London: Ekklesia), p. 79.
8 Joe Carter (2020) 'Should Christians sign non-disclosure agreements?', The Gospel Coalition, 28 May (available online at: www.thegospelcoalition.

org/article/should-christians-sign-non-disclosure-agreements>, accessed 5 October 2020).

9 Morgan Lee (2019) 'When Christian ministries ask their ex-employees not to talk', *Christianity Today*, 6 November (available online at: <www. christianitytoday.com/ct/2019/november-web-only/christian-ministries-non-disclosure-agreements-non-competes.html>, accessed 5 October 2020).

15 Holding ourselves accountable

1 Brené Brown (2015) *Daring Greatly: How the courage to be vulnerable transforms the way we live, love, parent, and lead* (London: Penguin Random House), p. 34.

2 Lisa Oakley and Justin Humphreys (2019) *Escaping the Maze of Spiritual Abuse: Creating healthy Christian cultures* (London: SPCK), pp. 139–40.

3 Mark and Cherith Stibbe (2019) *Restoring the Fallen: Creating safe spaces for those who fail* (Milton Keynes: Malcolm Down Publishing), p. 61.

4 Independent Inquiry: Child Sexual Abuse (2020) 'The Anglican Church: Safeguarding in the Church of England and Church in Wales', Investigation report, October (available online at: <www.iicsa.org.uk/key-documents/22519/view/anglican-church-investigation-report-6-october-2020.pdf>, accessed 27 February 2020), p. 80.

5 David Johnson and Jeff Van Vonderen (1991) *The Subtle Power of Spiritual Abuse* (Minneapolis, MN: Bethany House).

6 Scot McKnight and Laura Barringer (2020) *A Church Called Tov: Forming a goodness culture that resists abuses of power and promotes healing* (Carol Stream, IL: Tyndale), p. 16.

7 Chuck DeGroat (2020) *When Narcissism Comes to Church: Healing your community from emotional and spiritual abuse* (Downers Grove, IL: IVP, 2020), p. 103.

16 Just church

1 Rachel Held Evans (2018) *Inspired: Slaying giants, walking on water, and loving the Bible again.* (Nashville, TN: Thomas Nelson).

2 *Screwtape Proposes a Toast* by CS Lewis © copyright CS Lewis Pte Ltd 1959. Used with permission.

3 M. Craig Barnes (2001) *Sacred Thirst: Meeting God in the desert of our longings* (Grand Rapids, MI: Zondervan), p. 37.

4 The Justice Conference is a global movement encouraging thousands of Christ-followers to live out the message of Jesus and transform their communities by making justice a way of life. It takes place in seven countries

around the world, each engaging with issues relevant to its context and uniting thousands of Christians. The second UK conference was held from 21 to 22 February 2020 (see: <www.thejusticeconference.co.uk>, accessed 29 April 2020).

5 Robert Briner (1993) *Roaring Lambs: A gentle plan to radically change your world* (Grand Rapids, MI: Zondervan), p. 56.
6 Jude Padfield (2019) *Hopeful Influence: A theology of Christian leadership* (London: SCM Press), p. 225.
7 Edwin H. Friedman (2017) *A Failure of Nerve: Leadership in the age of the quick fix* (New York: Church Publishing), p.33–4.
8 Paula Gooder, *Body: Biblical spirituality for the whole person* (London: SPCK), pp. 108–9.

17 Just charity

1 John Stott (2006) *Issues Facing Christians Today* (Grand Rapids, MI: Zondervan), p. 225.
2 Ken Wytsma (2015) *The Grand Paradox: The messiness of life, the mystery of God and the necessity of faith* (Nashville, TN: Thomas Nelson), p. 46.
3 John Mark Comer (2015) *Garden City: Work, rest and the art of being human* (Grand Rapids, MI: Zondervan), p. 82.
4 Adrian Plass (1987) *Broken Windows, Broken Lives* (Chichester: Angel Press).
5 Sir Stephen Bubb (2017) 'The history of British charity', lecture delivered at New College, Oxford, 3 July (available online at: <https://charityfutures.org/wp-content/uploads/2019/01/history-of-charity-lecture-online-copy-30-6.pdf>, accessed 21 October 2020).
6 Data from the register of charities in England and Wales (available online at: <https://register-of-charities.charitycommission.gov.uk/charity-search>, accessed 21 October 2020).
7 Charity Commission for England and Wales (2018) 'Official statistics: Recent charity register statistics: Charity Commission', 18 October (available online at: <www.gov.uk/government/publications/charity-register-statistics/recent-charity-register-statistics-charity-commission>, accessed 21 October 2020).
8 Barna Group (2018) 'Christians who make a difference', a study commissioned by Tearfund in the UK and USA, p. 10.
9 Ken Costa (2016) *Know Your Why: Finding and Fulfilling Your Calling in Life* (Nashville, TN: Thomas Nelson, 2016).

10 Paula Gooder (2018) 'Why we do what we do', in 'The UK Church in Action: Perceptions of social justice and mission in a changing world' report (Barna/World Vision), p. 21.

11 'The public view: Charities do good work, but we don't like how some behave', *ThirdSector*, 18 September 2018 (available online at: <www.thirdsector.co.uk/public-view-charities-good-work-dont-behave/communications/article/1493061>, accessed 3 November 2020).

12 Stephen Delahunty (2020) 'Stories about spending at Kids Company were "salacious", High Court hears', *Third Sector*, 22 October (available online at: <www.thirdsector.co.uk/stories-spending-kids-company-salacious-high-court-hears/governance/article/1697998>, accessed 3 November 2020).

13 Charity Commission for England and Wales (2008; revised 2017) 'Guidance: Campaigning and political activity for charities (CC9)' (available online at: <https://assets.publishing.service.gov.uk/government/uploads/system/uploads/attachment_data/file/610137/CC9.pdf>, accessed 3 November 2020).

14 ACEVO (2017) 'Speaking frankly: Acting boldly', report, 1 May (available online at: <www.acevo.org.uk/reports/speaking-frankly-acting-boldly>, accessed 3 November 2020).

15 Meghan, J. Clark (2012) 'The complex but necessary union of charity and justice: Insights from the Vincentian tradition for contemporary Catholic social teaching', *Vincentian Heritage Journal*, DePaul University, 31 (2), 1, 1 November (available online at: <https://core.ac.uk/download/pdf/232975893.pdf>, accessed 27 February 2021).

16 Ken Costa, *Know Your Why*, p. 44.

18 Just business

1 Ken Wytsma (2013) *Pursuing Justice: The call to live and die for bigger things* (Nashville, TN: Thomas Nelson), p. 238.

2 Josephson Institute (2021) 'Fairness', Business Ethics blog (available online at: <https://josephsononbusinessethics.com/2010/12/fairness>, accessed 1 March 2021).

3 G. Demuijnck (2013) 'Duties of justice in business', in C. Luetge (eds) *Handbook of the Philosophical Foundations of Business Ethics* (Dordrecht: Springer, 2013), pp. 743–60.

4 Peter Bisanz (2014) 'How to make capitalism more ethical', World Economic Forum, 24 November (available online at: <www.weforum.org/agenda/2014/11/how-to-make-capitalism-more-ethical>, accessed 7 November 2020).

5 Gavin and Anne Calver (2020) *Unleashed: The ACTS Church today* (London: IVP), p. 166.

6 Calver, *Unleashed*, p. 167.

7 Jonathan Rushworth and Michael Schluter (2011) 'Transforming capitalism from within: A relational approach to the purpose, performance and assessment of companies', Relationships Foundation and Relationships Global, 26 October (available online at: <https://relationshipsfoundation. org/wp-content/uploads/2014/02/Transforming_Capitalism_Executive_ Summary.pdf>, accessed 1 March 2021).

8 David Brooks (2016) *The Road to Character* (London: Penguin), p. 267.

9 Edgar H. Schein and Peter A. Schein, *Humble Leadership: The power of relationships, openness and trust* (Oakland, CA: Berrett-Koehler), p. 34.

10 Brooks, *The Road to Character*, p. 59.

11 Christopher J. H. Wright (2006) *The Mission of God: Unlocking the Bible's grand narrative* (Nottingham: IVP), p. 418.

12 Ruth Valerio (2019) 'If you care about people, you have to care about the planet', *Evangelical Focus Europe*, 7 May (available online at: <https:// evangelicalfocus.com/science/4430/ruth-valerio-interview-environment- if-you-care-about-people-you-have-to-care-about-the-planet>, accessed 6 March 2021).

13 Tom Wright (n.d.) 'Beginning to think about the new creation' (available online at: <www.ntwrightonline.org/beginning-to-think-about-the-new- creation>, accessed September 2020).

14 Center for Economic and Social Justice (n.d.) 'What is Justice-Based Management(sm)?' (available online at: <www.cesj.org/what-is-justice- based-management>, accessed 1 March 2021).

15 Lily Zheng (2020) 'We're entering the age of corporate social justice', *Harvard Business Review*, 15 June (available online at: <https://hbr.org/2020/06/were- entering-the-age-of-corporate-social-justice>, accessed 1 March 2021).

16 Karen L. Newman (1993) 'The just organization: Creating and maintaining justice in work environments', *Washington and Lee Law Review*, 50 (4), Article 8, 1 September (available online at: <https://scholarlycommons. law.wlu.edu/cgi/viewcontent.cgi?article=1784&context=wlulr>, accessed 1 March 2021).

17 OpenStax resource (n.d.) 'Loyalty to the company', Business Ethics (B C Campus Open Publishing) (available online at: <https://opentextbc.ca/ businessethicsopenstax/chapter/a-theory-of-justice>, accessed 1 March 2021).

18 Josephson Institute (2021) 'Fairness', Business Ethics blog (available online at: <https://josephsononbusinessethics.com/2010/12/fairness>, accessed 1 March 2021).

19 Jonathan Rushworth and Michael Schluter, 'Transforming capitalism from within'.

19 Just society

1 Catechism of the Catholic Church (1912), quoted in *Pontifical Council for Justice and Peace (2004) Compendium of the Social Doctrine of the Church*, Chapter 4: Principles of the Church's social doctrine (Rome: Vatican) on CatholicCulture.org's website (available online at: <https://catholicculture.org/culture/library/view.cfm?id=7214>, accessed 3 November 2020).

2 Pierre Elliott Trudeau, Ron Graham (ed.) (1999) 'The just society', *The Essential Trudeau* (Toronto: McClelland & Stewart), pp. 16–20 (available online at: <www.edu.gov.mb.ca/k12/cur/socstud/foundation_gr6/blms/6-4-4a.pdf>, accessed 21 October 2020).

3 Ken Wytsma (2013) *Pursuing Justice: The call to live and die for bigger things* (Nashville, TN: Thomas Nelson), p. 7.

4 The Archbishop of Canterbury, Justin Welby (2019) 'Archbishop of Canterbury delivers William Temple Foundation Annual Lecture', 14 May (available online at: <www.archbishopofcanterbury.org/speaking-and-writing/speeches/archbishop-canterbury-delivers-william-temple-foundation-annual-lecture>, accessed 21 October 2020).

5 Andrew Bradstock (2013) 'Prosperity and justice', *The Victoria University of Wellington Law Review* (available online at: <https://togetherforthecommongood.co.uk/leading-thinkers/prosperity-and-justice>, accessed on 1 March 2021).

6 *Pontifical Council for Justice and Peace (2004) Compendium of the Social Doctrine of the Church*, Chapter 4, Section II: The principle of the common good (Rome: Vatican) (available online at: <www.vatican.va/roman_curia/pontifical_councils/justpeace/documents/rc_pc_justpeace_doc_20060526_compendio-dott-soc_en.html>, accessed on 1 March 2021). Principle to be found in the Second Vatican Council document *Gaudium et spes* (1965).

7 Adapted from Michael Sandel (2010) 'Towards a just society', *The Guardian*, 20 February (available online at: <www.theguardian.com/commentisfree/2010/feb/20/just-society-civic-virtues>, accessed 21 October 2020).

8 Mac Pier (2012) *Consequential Leadership* (Downers Grove, IL: IVP), p. 196.

9 N. T. Wright (2007) 'Kingdom come: The public meaning of the Gospels', Jason Goroncy's blog (available online at: <https://jasongoroncy.com/2008/06/17/nt-wright-kingdom-come-the-public-meaning-of-the-gospels>, accessed 1 March 2021).